Anonymus

A Catalogue of the pictures at Weston

Belonging to the Earl of Bradford

Anonymus

A Catalogue of the pictures at Weston
Belonging to the Earl of Bradford

ISBN/EAN: 9783741177774

Manufactured in Europe, USA, Canada, Australia, Japa

Cover: Foto ©Thomas Meinert / pixelio.de

Manufactured and distributed by brebook publishing software
(www.brebook.com)

Anonymus

A Catalogue of the pictures at Weston

A Catalogue

Of the

Pictures at Weston,

Belonging to

The Earl of Bradford.

1895.

" The pencil speaks the tongue of every land."

Dryden.

This Catalogue is compiled from a list of the pictures at Weston, carefully made out by the Earl of Bradford in 1885.

The following lists have been referred to :—

Weston Catalogue of Orlando, first Earl of Bradford.

Weston Catalogue of 1837, made out by Georgina Elizabeth, Countess of Bradford.

The "Torrington" and "Newport" Catalogues of 1719.

George Griffiths,

Weston-under-Lizard.

The numbers in this Catalogue correspond with the numbers on the pictures.

The terms "right" and "left" are those of the spectator, unless otherwise mentioned.

The sizes given are the sight measurements of the canvas.

The Biographical Catalogue referred to is that of the Portraits at Weston, edited by Miss Mary Boyle, and published by Elliot Stock in 1888. *Grossly Inaccurate*

The Illustrations are Photogravure plates engraved by Messrs. John Steen & Co., of Wolverhampton from photographs taken by Mr. Bowler, of Oakengates, Salop.

Catalogue of Pictures.

1

Half length. Leaning on her left hand. In mourning.

23in. high × 19in. wide.

Rachel, Lady Russell. $\text{BORN} \quad \text{DIED}$ 1637—1728

Widow of the patriot, Lord Russell. Second daughter of Thomas, last Earl of Southampton of the Wriothesley family, first married, probably in 1653 to Lord Vaughan, son of the Earl of Carberry, and afterwards to William Lord Russell, second son of William, 5th Earl, and 1st Duke of Bedford. During Lord Russell's trial, in 1683, Lady Rachel assisted him in open court by taking notes of the evidence, and, after his condemnation, afforded him unfailing comfort and support. Her letters have been published.

2

Oval. Tawny and blue dress.

28 high × 24 wide.

Lady Robert Russell. *By Sir Godfrey Kneller.*

Daughter of Edward Russell, and widow of Thomas Cheek, of Pirgo, county Sussex. She married her cousin Lord Robert Russell.

3

Scarlet & ermine robes, gold chain, close cap: left hand holds gloves.

49 high × 39 wide.

Sir Orlando Bridgeman, Lord Chief Justice, afterwards Lord Keeper.

1609—1674. *By Riley.*

Son of Dr. John Bridgeman, Bishop of Chester, by Elizabeth, daughter of Dr. Helyar, Canon of Exeter and Archdeacon of Barnstaple. He married, first, Judith, daughter and sole heir of John Kynaston, Esq., of Morton Hall, county Salop, which became his father the Bishop's place of refuge during the Usurpation. By this marriage he left a son, Sir John Bridgeman, of Castle Bromwich, 2nd Bart., and a daughter, Elizabeth, who died young. Sir Orlando married secondly, Dorothy, daughter of Dr. Saunders, Provost of Oriel College, Oxford, and relict of George Cradock, Esq., of Caverswall Castle, county Stafford, by whom he left two sons and three daughters, viz :—Sir Orlando Bridgeman, created a Baronet, of Ridley, county Chester, by King Charles II., 1673, and Sir Francis of Teddington, Sergeant-at-Law, knighted by King Charles II. One daughter, Charlotte, married Sir Thos. Myddleton, of Chirk Castle, Bart. ; the other two daughters died young.

At the commencement of the Long Parliament, Orlando Bridgeman was returned for the Borough of Wigan in Lancashire.

He was one of the few who voted against the attainder of Lord Strafford, on whose behalf he made a short but manly appeal. When the Civil War broke out Orlando Bridgeman did not indeed, as was the case with several lawyers, throw aside the gown for the sword; but he went into the north, and in the City of Chester, and elsewhere, did the King good service by affording the royal troops all the assistance in his power, in co-operation with his father, the Bishop of the Diocese. Clarendon tells us how "the city of Chester remained true to his "Majesty, influenced thereto by the credit and example of Bishop John Bridgeman, "and the reputation and dexterity of his son Orlando, a lawyer of very good "estimation." For these proofs of loyalty he was expelled the House of Commons, and the Bishop's estates sequestrated. But when Charles summoned the members of both Houses that had been faithful to him, to his own Parliament at Oxford, Orlando Bridgeman took his seat as member for Wigan, 1640; he became Lord Chief Baron of the Exchequer, 2nd June, 1660, and was created a Baronet same month.

During the *interregnum* he refused to put on his gown or to plead, but contented himself with acting as a conveyancer or chamber counsel. Yet we are informed that he took great note of passing events, whether judicial or political, and that though he prudently abstained from any small plot hatching in the King's name, which he considered would be prejudicial to the royal cause, yet to the great measures which affected the Restoration our lawyer gave his strong adherence, and rejoiced in the return of Charles the Second to England.

He had quick promotion, being made Sergeant-at-Law, Lord Chief Baron of the Exchequer, and Speaker of the House of Lords in the absence of the Lord Chancellor. His conduct on the trial of the regicides has naturally been differently judged, according to the bias of party feeling, but at all events his eloquence in charging the jury was highly extolled at the time, and when he had concluded, the applause was so great that Judge Bridgeman felt himself called upon to check the expression thereof, saying: "that it was more suitable for the audience of a stage play rather than a court of justice."

On the expiration of the trials, Bridgeman was made a Baronet and Chief Justice of the Common Pleas; and it was said of him that while presiding in this Court his reputation was at its zenith, and "his moderation and equity were such that he seemed to carry a chancery in his breast."

In 1667 he was appointed Lord-Keeper of the Great Seal of England, but being supplanted by the Earl of Shaftesbury, Sir Orlando retired to his villa, near Teddington, where he died and was buried.

ROGER NORTH said:—"He was a celebrated lawyer, and sat with high esteem in the place of Chief Justice of the Common Pleas."

LORD ELLENBOROUGH extols him as an eminent judge, distinguished by the profundity of his learning and the extent of his industry. There is no doubt that the name of Sir Orlando Bridgeman, Lord-Keeper of the Great Seal, continues to be honoured not only in the annals of his own family, but in the learned profession of the Law.—*Mary Boyle's Biography.*

Another Biographer says:—"This great and good man was a glory to his family and indeed to the country at large."

4

Oval. Lace collar, loose brown cloak.

28in. high × 25in. wide.

Lord Robert Russell. (Died 1722.) *By Sir Godfrey Kneller.*

Fifth son of the first Duke of Bedford, by Anne Carr, daughter of the Earl of Somerset. He married his cousin (*see No. 2*), by whom he had no children. He served in seven Parliaments for Tavistock.

5

In profile. Elizabethan collar, brown cloak.

18in. × 15

Hugo Grotius, when a boy. (1583—1645-6.) *By Mirevelt.*

Hugo de Groot, son of John de Groot (Dutch for "Great").

Bio. Cata. p. 19.

6

In armour. Brown sleeve, long white tie.

26in. × 20

The Hon. Col. Andrew Newport. (1622—1699.) *By Sir Godfrey Kneller.*

Son of Lord Newport, the noted Royalist, by Rachel, daughter of Sir John Levison, Knight, and sister of Sir Richard Levison, K.B., of Trentham. Col. Newport was a Commissioner of Customs.

Bio. Cata. p. 19.

7

Left figure, aged and grey, extends left hand towards disciple on the right; right figure younger, shaven; central figure with beard, and hand in his bosom.

65in. × 50

St. Peter, St. James, and St. John. *By Caravaggio.*

8

Grey and brown.

49in. × 49

Two Horses. *By Stubbs.*

9

Earl on the left, black robe, square collar, left hand holding letter. The Secretary, in red, writing.

57in. × 50

Thomas Wentworth, Earl of Strafford, and his Secretary. *After Vandyke.*

(1593-4, executed 1641.)

Friend and Counsellor of Charles I.

10

Oval. Brown coat, embroidered sleeve.

28in. × 24

Col. The Hon. John Russell. *By Sir Godfrey Kneller.*

Third son of Francis, fourth Earl of Bedford. He served with distinction in the Royal Army under Charles I., and died 1681. His sister Diana married Francis, Lord Newport, and was afterwards Countess of Bradford.

Bio. Cata. p. 43.

11

In black, square cut collar.

15in. high × 12in. wide.

Francis Russell, Fourth Earl of Bedford. (Died 1641.)

By Remé.

Only son of William Russell, "the heroic Baron of Thornhaugh." He married Catherine, daughter and co-heiress of Giles Bridges, third Lord Chandos. He exerted himself greatly to save Lord Strafford, and died universally mourned. He was father of the first Countess of Bradford.

Bio. Cata. p. 44.

12

Old man in profile to the left, holds book, turns leaves, boy on right.

48in. × 89

Seneca instructing Nero.

Spanish School.

13

In armour.

25in. × 20

William, Lord Russell. (1689, executed 1688.) *By Russell.*

The Patriot. Eldest surviving son of William, fifth Earl, and first Duke of Bedford. He married Lady Rachel, daughter of the Earl of Southampton (*see No. 1*). Rapin says, "the verdict of Guilty was the most crying injustice that ever was perpetrated in England."

Bio. Cata. p. 48.

14

Bust. Close black cap, black gown, white square collar.

24in. × 21

William Harvey, M.D. (1578—1657-8.)

Doctor Harvey, son of Thomas Harvey, of Folkstone, in Kent. A celebrated Physician. The discoverer of the circulation of the blood.

He accompanied the Earl of Arundel, his patron and friend, to Germany, &c. Cromwell destroyed his furniture and all his papers, "which love nor money could replace."

Bio. Cata. p. 57.

15

Youth in armour, yellow sash.

15in. × 12

The Hon. Edward Russell. (Died 1665.) *By Remé.*

Youngest son of Francis, fourth Earl of Bedford.

Bio. Cata. p. 65.

16

In armour. Blue sash, jewel. Oval shewn on canvas

30in. × 24

William Russell, Fifth Earl, First Duke of Bedford. *By Sir Godfrey Kneller.*

(1613—1700.)

Eldest son of Francis, fourth Earl of Bedford. K.G. 1672, created Duke of Bedford, 1694. He married Anne Carr, only child of the Earl and Countess of Somerset.

Bio. Cata. p. 66.

17

Grey coat, orange scarf
with jewel.

26in. high × 20in. wide.

Sir Thomas Myddleton, died 1683 *By Russell.*

Second Baronet of Chirk Castle. Son of Sir Thomas Myddleton, first Bart. He married, first, Elizabeth, daughter and co-heir of Sir Thomas Wilbraham, and secondly, Charlotte, (*see No. 159*), daughter of Sir Orlando Bridgeman, Bart., and had an only daughter Charlotte, (*see No. 198*), married first to Edward, Earl of Warwick, and secondly to the Right Hon. Joseph Addison, the Poet.

18

Bust. Youth in armour.
Green sash.

14in. × 11

The Hon. Francis Russell. died 1641 *By Remé.*

Second son of Francis, fourth Earl of Bedford. Married Catherine, daughter of Lord Grey de Wark, and widow of Sir Edward Moseley, Bart., and of the Lord North and Grey. Brother of the first Countess of Bradford.

Bio. Cata. p. 71.

19

As a boy, half-length,
pink on shoulder, blue
girdle.

20in. × 17

Prince Maurice as Cupid. (1620—1653) *By Honthorst.*

Fourth son of Frederick Elector Palatine, by Elizabeth, Princess of England, daughter of James I., the famous commander and companion in arms of Prince Rupert, *see No. 48.*

Bio. Cata. p. 75.

20

Madonna on left in red,
white over her head;
leans over Child, from
whom she is removing a
veiling. Child holds a
plate with an apple
thereon.

35½in. × 28½

A Madonna with Sleeping Child. *By Gio. André de Ferrari.*

21

Joseph on the left, in
yellow, bareheaded, with
staff. Virgin seated on a
mule, going to the right.
The Saviour rests in her
lap.

19in. × 26

The Flight into Egypt. *By Castiglione.*

22

The Saviour on the left
in grey and red: St. John
looking at the Saviour.

14½in. × 20

Our Saviour and St. John. *By Peter van Lindt.*

This picture was once cut into two and framed separately, but has now been restored to its original state.

23

A man, women, cattle, and sheep; man on horse-back approaching.
48½in. high × 38in. wide

Landscape.

By Berghem.

24

Blue cloak, hands in the attitude of prayer.
30in. × 25

A Madonna.

By Sasso Ferrato.

25

Lady on a white horse another on a cream one, man alongside, boy driving cows and goats; two packhorses.
28¾in. × 25½

Landscape.

By Bout and Bodewyns.

26

Cloak and doublet. Left hand gloved with white glove, and holding the other; large white cuffs, turned back; deep white collar and tassels.
42in. × 34

Colonel West.

By Walker.

A distinguished Parliamentarian Officer; he was engaged in Inverkeithing fight, 1651.

27

Bare rocky place, river; man with long cap and book; a cross near.

A Landscape, with a Philosopher Studying.

By Joachim Patenier.

28

In red, slashed black; partly in armour, stands over a prostrate form: battle axe, belt, shoes.

A Swiss brandishing his Sword.

By Bol.

29

Cattle, goats, two people, dog, fording a river; donkey with panniers leading the way.
9½in. × 12¾

A Landscape.

By Berghem.

30

Oval. Cadmus advances
drawing sword; two
other figures.
5in. high × 4¼in. wide.

Cadmus and the Dragon. *By Paul Brill.*

31

Eight figures gambling,
outside a Cottage.
9in. × 7¼

A Game of Rouge et Noir. *By Molenaer.*

(Or "a Dutch Drol.")

32

Small panel. Five
figures.
12¾in. × 10

Inside of a Cabaret. *By Brower.*

Called "a man with his Back to ye Fire," in the Torrington Catalogue.

33

The mouth of a river
with two ships and
numerous boats.
40½in. × 60

A Sea Piece. *By Abraham Stork.*

34

Seated, looking towards
the left; wand, blue
ribbon, and Star of the
Garter.
44in. × 87

Thomas Wriothesley, Earl of Southampton.

(died 1667). *By Sir Peter Lely.*

Second, but only surviving son of the third Earl, by Elizabeth, daughter of John Vernon, of Hodnet. He was father of Lady Rachel Russell, (*See No. 1*), the friend of Essex, the patron of Shakespeare, and one of the four last friends allowed to remain with Charles I. Later he became Lord High Treasurer to Charles II., and was created a K.G.

35

On panel.
11¼in. × 10

A Music Lesson. *By W. Mieris.*

36

8in. × 6½

Topers. *By Teniers.*

37

Oval. Seated figure; cap
with feather and pearls,
chains round her neck.
9½in. × 7

An Old Woman, with an Hour-Glass.

By Gerard Dow.

This is believed to be a portrait of the Artist's Mother.

38

Oval.
4in. high × 5½in. wide.

Danæ and the Golden Shower. *By J. Rothenhamer.*

39

The Lady at a table, in
a white dress.
11¼in. × 10

An Offer rejected. *By W. Mieris.*

40

Small, on Copper.
Figure seated, with a
book in her lap.
9¼in. × 7½

A Sybil. *By Schidone.*

41

Half-length; crowned;
her left hand extended;
blue and red drapery.
44½in. × 35

St. Catherine. *By E. Sirani.*

42

A creek, banditti, boat,
and castle.
28in. × 38

A Landscape with Figures. *By Salvator Rosa.*

43

Virgin, in blue, kneeling
and reading, angel
holding lilies.
29½in. × 15½

The Annunciation. *By C. J. Ratti.*

44

14in. × 12

The Crucifixion. *By Bernardo Strozzi.*
(called "Il Capucino").

45

Each panel
4½in. × 3¼

Eight Subjects from the History of our Saviour.
By Flavio Minaresi).
(Four panels, sub-divided).

1.—The Meeting of Elizabeth and Mary, and the Birth of Christ.
2.—The Circumcision, and the Adoration of Wise Men.
3.—The Betrayal, and the Scourge.
4.—The Crucifixion, and the Descent from the Cross.

46

Slashed doublet, long fair
hair.
42in. high × 33½ wide.

Colonel, afterwards Lord Goring.   *After Vandyck.*

(died 1662, v.p.)

Son of Sir George Goring, Kt., afterwards Baron Goring and Earl of Norwich.

Bio. Cata. p. 80.

47

Drove of Cattle and Goats
crossing a bridge, several
figures.
31in. × 41

A Landscape.   *By Claude Lorraine.*

48

Bust, a pink sash over
shoulders.
20in. × 17

Prince Rupert, as Mars.   *By Houthorst.*

(1619—1682.)

Third son of Frederick Elector Palatine, and King of Bohemia, by Princess Elizabeth of England, daughter of James I.

Bio. Cata. p. 83.

49

The Virgin on a mule.
14in. × 11

The Flight into Egypt.   *By Filippo Lauri.*

50

Nymph in red, escaping
from a man in blue,
riding upon an eagle.
11in. × 9¼

Jupiter and Io.   *By Filippo Lauri.*

51

Elizabethan ruff.
Elaborate lace head-dress,
rich frock, coral and bells.
Holds a card.
35in. × 27½

Lady Diana Russell, first Countess of Bradford, as a child.   (Died 1694).

Youngest daughter of Francis, fourth Earl of Bedford; married Francis Newport, first Earl of Bradford.

52

The Saviour in blue.
Mary, on the left, with
hands outstretched.
22½in. × 19

"Noli Me tangere."   *By Carlo Maratti.*

53
On Copper.
The Virgin on the right,
In red!; three angels In
a stable.
11in. high × 8½in. wide.

The Adoration of the Angels,

54
Venus reclining In a grove ;
Cupid and doves.
11½in. × 9¼

Venus and Cupid.

By Filippo Lauri.

55
In a blue silk dress,
gathering a lily.
35in. × 29

Lady Isabella Dormer, afterwards Countess of Mountrath (as a child, 8 years old).

By Sir Peter Lely.

Second daughter of Charles, third Lord Dormer, and second and last Earl of Carnarvon of that family. Married Sir Charles Coote, fourth Earl of Mountrath.

Bio. Cata. p. 95.

56
Oval. Bust, In blue dress,
dark hair.
28in. × 24½

Lady Diana Fielding.

By Sir Peter Lely.

(died 1781).

She was daughter of Francis Newport, first Earl of Bradford, by Lady Diana Russell. Married first, Thomas Howard, of Ashstead, Surrey, Esq., K.B. ; secondly, Hon. William Fielding, younger son of William, fifth Earl of Denbigh, and second Earl of Desmond.

Bio. Cata. p. 96.

57
Oval. Blue gown, fair
curls.
28in. × 24

Diana, Viscountess Newport, afterwards Countess of Bradford. (1622—1694.)

By Verelst.

Youngest daughter of Francis, Earl of Bedford.

58
Brown dress and blue scarf.
Seated, leaning her arm
on a boulder.
48in. × 40

A Lady.

By Sir Peter Lely.

59
Brown silk dress and scarf.
49in. × 39

A Lady.

By Sir Peter Lely.

In one catalogue this picture is called 'Mrs. Roberts."

60
Undress Guards' Uniform.
35in. high × 27in. wide.

The Hon. Orlando Bridgeman *By Sir George Hayter.*
(1794—1827.)

Grenadier Guards.   Third son of first Earl of Bradford.
Married Lady Selina Nèedham, daughter of Francis, first Earl of Kilmorey.

Bio. Cata. p. 102.

61
In naval uniform, white vest, holding a telescope.
35in. × 27

Captain the Hon. Charles Bridgeman, R.N.
(1791—1860.)   *By Sir George Hayter.*

Second son of Orlando, first Earl of Bradford.   Married Eliza Caroline, daughter of Sir Henry Chamberlain, Bart.   He was a Vice-Admiral.

62
Hair in curls; holding a dog.
11in. × 9

The Hon. Selina Forester, afterwards Countess of Bradford.   *By Sir Francis Grant.*

Youngest daughter of the first Baron Forester and Lady Katherine Manners, daughter of the fourth Duke of Rutland.   Married in 1844 Viscount Newport, afterwards Earl of Bradford.

Bio. Cata. p. 103.

63
Black sleeves, edged with ermine, gilt collar, black cap, and jewel : putting on a ring.
9in. × 7

Portrait.   (Unknown.)

64
Black, white vest.
12in. × 9

Robert Jenkinson, 2nd Earl of Liverpool.
(1770—1828.)   *By Sir George Hayter.*

Prime Minister, 1812 to 1827.   Son of Charles, first Earl of Liverpool.   Married, first, Lady Louisa Hervey, third daughter of the Bishop of Derry, fourth Earl of Bristol ; secondly, Mary, daughter of Charles Chester, Esq. (formerly Bagot), brother of the first Lord Bagot.

Bio. Cata. p. 104.

65
In blue uniform.
10in. × 8

Napoleon Buonaparte, the first Emperor of France.   *By David.*
Bio. Cata. p. 107.

66

White Waistcoat, cloak.
86in. high × 27in. wide.

George Augustus Frederick Henry, second Earl of Bradford. (1789—1865.) *By Sir George Hayter.*

Eldest son of Orlando, first Earl. Married, first, Georgina, daughter of Sir Thomas Moncreiffe, Bart.; secondly, Helen, widow of Sir David Moncreiffe, Bart, and daughter of Æneas Mackay, Esq.

Bio. Cata. p. 108.

67

18in. × 11

Queen Anne Boleyn. *A Sketch, by Holbein.*

(With memorandum in his own handwriting.)

Executed 1536. Daughter of Thomas, Earl of Wiltshire and Ormonde, created Marchioness of Pembroke. Second wife of King Henry VIII.

Bio. Cata. p. 108.

68

Black, scarlet robes.
86in. × 27

Orlando, first Earl of Bradford. *By Sir G. Hayter.* (1762—1825.)

Eldest son of Sir Henry Bridgeman, first Baron Bradford. Married the Hon. Lucy Elizabeth Byng, daughter and co-heir of George, fourth Viscount Torrington.

Bio. Cata. p. 109.

69

Oval. Widow's cap.
18in. × 11

Her Majesty Queen Victoria. *By Thomas.*

A Sketch, executed for Lord Bradford when Lord Chamberlain, by Her Majesty's permission.

70

In red : Ribbon of the Garter.
18in. × 14

King George II. *By Pine.*

Born 1683. King, 1727—1760.

71

9in. × 7

Taking down from the Cross. *By Palma Vecchio.*

72

In black, full length, holding the string of eyeglass ; white waistcoat.
17in. × 10

Edward Stanley, 14th Earl of Derby, K.G. (1799—1869.) *By Sir Francis Grant, P.R.A.*

Eldest son of Edward, 13th Earl. Married Emma Caroline, daughter of Edward, first Lord Skelmersdale.

A small portrait in oils, painted from the life by *Sir Francis Grant, P.R.A.*, being the original study for a large portrait.

(Given to Lord Bradford by the Artist.)

Bio. Cata. p. 110.

73

In blue and red.
7in. × 6

Virgin and Child, with St. John. *By Sotto Cleve.*

74

Fur trimmed coat.
80in. high × 24in. wide.

H. Greswold Lewis, Esq. *By Constable.*

Of Malvern Hall.   Died 1819.   Married the Hon. Charlotte, daughter of Henry Lord Bradford.

75

Black coat. White tie.
80in. × 24

The Hon. & Rev. George Bridgeman. *By Constable.*

(1765—1882).

Youngest son of Henry Lord Bradford.   Married first, Lady Lucy Boyle; secondly, Charlotte Louisa, daughter of Wm. Poyntz, Esq. Late Rector of Weston and Wigan.

Bio. Cata. p. 111.

76

Brown coat.
White waistcoat.
31in. × 25

The Hon. John Bridgeman Simpson. *After Hoppner.*

(1763—1850).

Second son of Henry Lord Bradford, by the daughter and heir of the Rev. John Simpson, of Babworth.   Married first, Henrietta Frances, daughter and heir of Sir Thomas Worsley, Bart.   Assumed the maternal arms and name of Simpson 1785.   He married, secondly, Grace, daughter of Samuel Estwicke, Esq.

(The original of this picture is at Babworth).

Bio. Cata. p. 114.

77

In dark coat. White
neck-cloth.
29in. × 24

Sir George Gunning, Bart. *By J. Jackson.*

(1783—1823).

Eldest son of Sir Robert Gunning, Bart., who was Ambassador at Berlin and St. Petersburg.   Married the younger daughter of Henry Lord Bradford.

Bio. Cata. p. 114.

78

Right hand in fold of
coat. White frill.
80in. × 24

Sir William Lowther, Bart. *By Sir Joshua Reynolds.*

(died 1763 ?).

Son of Sir Thomas Lowther, of Holker Hall, by Lady Elizabeth Cavendish, ("Lady Betty"), daughter of the 2nd Duke of Devonshire. Unmarried.

Bio. Cata. p. 114.

79

Naval Uniform.
30in. high × 24in. wide.

Lord Hugh Seymour, Vice-Admiral. *By Hoppner.*

(1759—1801).

Fifth son of Francis, Earl, afterwards Marquis of Hertford, by a daughter of the Duke of Grafton. Married Horatia, daughter of James, 2nd Earl Waldegrave, one of the "Three Graces" in the picture by Sir Joshua Reynolds.

Bio. Cata. p. 115.

80

Peer's scarlet robes.
White hair.
30in. × 24

Henry, 1st Lord Bradford. *By Romney.*

(1725—1800).

Sir Henry Bridgeman, Bart., of Castle Bromwich, created Baron Bradford, 1794. Married Elizabeth, daughter and sole heir of the Rev. John Simpson of Stoke Hall, Co. Derby.

Bio. Cata. p. 117, 188.

81

Uniform of Grenadier
Guards.
30in. × 24

Mr. George Bridgeman, Grenadier Guards.

(1727—1767). *By Sir Joshua Reynolds.*

Third son of Sir Orlando Bridgeman, and Lady Anne Newport. Died unmarried.

82

Naval Uniform.
30in. × 24

Admiral Payne. *By Hoppner.*

(1752—1803).

Equerry to the Prince of Wales. Captain John Willett Payne, R.N. afterwards Vice-Admiral.

Bio. Cata. p. 118.

83

When a child. In a red
frock, sitting on the
lawn.
33in. × 35

The Hon. Orlando George Charles Bridgeman.

By Sir George Hayter.

Third Earl of Bradford; born 1819. Married the Hon. Selina Louisa Forester, (*see No. 62*), youngest daughter of the first Lord Forester.

Bio. Cata. p. 119.

84

Red brown dress; the
child in white.
3in. high x 39in. wide.

Margaret Howard, Countess of Carlisle, and Her Niece.
By Stone, after Vandyck.

She was the third daughter of Francis, fourth Earl of Bedford. Married first, at a very early age, James Hay, afterwards second Earl of Carlisle ; secondly, Robert Rich, Earl of Warwick, second Earl of Holland ; thirdly, Edward Montague, Earl of Manchester. Born 1618 ; died 1664. Her niece was Lady Diana Russell.

(See Bio. Cata. p. 123, and see Woburn Catalogue No. 133, No. 134, and No. 135.)

Howard ?

85

The Virgin in red and
blue.
32in. x 20

The Flight into Egypt.
By G. Raf. Badaracco.

86

In armour, holding a
baton ; the child in
red.
57in. x 50

The Earl of Arundel and Surrey, and one of his Grandsons.
By Sir A. Vandyck.

(1592—1646.)

Thomas Howard, only son of Philip, Earl of Arundel, who died a prisoner in the Tower. Restored to the Earldom and Estates 1 James I., and to the Earldom of Surrey. Created Earl Marshal 1621, and Earl of Norfolk, 1644.

(*There is a similar picture in the Duke of Norfolk's Collection.*)
Bio. Cata. p. 124.

87

86½in. x 20

Hippomenes and Atalanta.
By F. Albano.

88

a crimson dress, pointing
with right hand ; loose
white sleeves ; pearl
necklace.
49in. x 39

Dorothy, Countess of Sunderland.
By Vandyck.

(1620—1684.)

The "Sacharissa" of Waller, renowned for her beauty. The eldest daughter of Robert Sidney, Earl of Leicester, by Dorothy, daughter of Henry Percy, ninth Earl of Northumberland. She married Henry, Lord Spencer, of Wormleighton, created Earl of Sunderland, 1643.
Bio. Cata. p. 125.

89

32in. x 20

The Angel appearing to Joseph in a Dream.
By G. R. Badaracco.

90

Three portraits, viz.—
Front face, and right and
left profiles.
42in. high × 33in. wide.

Charles I., King of England.

(1600—1649.) *By Carlo Maratti, after Vandyck.*

Second son of James I. Married Henrietta Maria of France.

(The original, by Vandyck, is at Windsor Castle.)

91

Red wings, right arm
over his head.
24½in. × 14

A Cherub. *By Paul Veronese.*

92

Back to the spectator.
19½in. × 13½

Cupid shaving his Bow. *After Correggio.*

93

Standing upon a globe:
holds a red flower.
24¾in. × 14

A Cherub. *By Paul Veronese.*

94

16 parrots, and other
birds.
18½in. × 13

Birds. *By Van Kessel or " Boon."*

95

Red dress, long sleeves.
39in. × 20

A Venetian Courtesan. *By Paul Veronese.*

96

On panel, 8 figures.
11½in. × 14

The Judgment of Paris. *By Poëlemburg.*

97

On panel. Bust, looking
to left; flat black cap
with feather, light coat,
double chain, small ruff.
13in. × 9½

Sir Edward Seymour, afterwards Duke of Somerset. *By Holbein.*

Executed 1552. Second, but eldest surviving son of Sir John Seymour, of Wulfhall, Co. Wilts, by Margaret, daughter of Sir John Wentworth. On the King's marriage with Jane Seymour, his sister, he was created Viscount Beauchamp, and Earl of Hertford, 1537. Created Duke by Edward VI., in whose reign he was " The Protector."

Bio. Cata. p. 131.

98
Scene in front of a Palace.
12in. × 16¾

Esther and Ahasuerus. *By Ehrenburg.*

-

99
Black gown, splendidly embroidered; pearls, rings; hands joined; curious coiffure; diagonals in gold.
18½in. × 13

A Lady. *By Lucas Cranach.*

"Kranach was born in 1470; he resided many years at the Court of the Elector of Saxony, and this, from the richness of her dress, is probably a portrait of the Electress, or some other distinguished Lady of that Court."—*1837 Catalogue.*

100
Trees, river, boat, and figures.
16¼in. × 20¾

A Moonlight Scene. *By Vanderneer.*

101
Red robe. Rose in right hand.
30in. × 32

A Lady, with a Monkey and a Flower Pot.
By Paris Bordone.
("By Giorgione."—Newport Catalogue.)

102
On copper. Dancing.
6 other figures.
11in. × 27

A Nymph and Satyr. *By Poëlemburg.*

103
On panel. Other figures and cherubs.
12¼in. × 18½

Venus giving Arms to Æneas. *Venetian School.*

104
On a charger.
18in. × 21¼

The Head of John the Baptist.

105
In a green frock, looking towards the right; red coral necklet and bracelets.
88½in. × 26

Portrait of a Child. *By Paul Veronese.*

106
Circular.
13in. diameter.

Vandyck, as Paris. *After Vandyck.*

107
68in. × 97½

A Larder Scene, with Dogs. *By Snyders.*

NOTE.—The puppies were not to be seen some years ago, having been painted out, but on the picture being cleaned they were brought to light again.

108
In a yellow frock, white sleeves.
33½in. × 26.

Portrait of a Child. *By Paul Veronese.*

109
Circular.
Brown coat, white vest, black hat, white feather.
13in. diameter.

Sir Nicholas Carew. *By Holbein.*

110
Looking down; white collar, beard, and moustache.
19in. × 14½

An Old Man's Head. *By Vandyck.*

111
Brown coat: small eyes, looking straight.
18in. × 18½

A Man's Head. *By Tintoretto.*

112
A ship, tower, wreckage, and figures.
39in. × 52

A Storm. *By Joseph Vernet.*

(From the Earl of Mountrath's Collection.)

113
In white and blue, holding a nosegay; a table beside her.
44in. × 36.

The Countess of Oxford. *By Vandyck.*

Beatrix Van Hemmend, a Dutch lady, of Friesland ; married Robert de Vere, 19th Earl of Oxford, who died 1632.

Bio. Cata. p. 141.

114
Figures, donkey, ladder,
&c., near a shed and fire.
17¼in. high × 35in. wide

A Winter Scene. *By Francesco Bassano.*

115
On Copper.
6in. × 8½

St. Peter walking on the Sea. *By J. Breughel.*

116
Head and shoulders,
looking towards left;
dark hair, light
moustache and beard.
19½in. × 16

Portrait of a Gentleman. *By Titian.*
Unknown.

117
Large hat, fur cape,
holding a pipe.
19½in. × 16

A Piper. *By Piazetti, after Giorgione.*

118
Ship in harbour, net
being drawn in.
38in. × 52

A Calm. *By J. Vernet.*
(From the Earl of Mountrath's Collection).

119
Half length, in black
robes, looking to left;
astronomical globe by
his side.
41½in. × 36

Sir Kenelm Digby. *By Vandyck.*
(1603—1665).

Son of Sir Everard Digby, who suffered death in 1606 for his concern in the Gunpowder Treason. Born at Gothurst, the property of his mother, the daughter and heir of Sir William Malsho. An accomplished gentleman, philosopher, courtier, soldier, and one of the ornaments of the Court of Charles I. He married the beautiful Venetia, daughter of Sir Edward Stanley, K.B., of Tong Castle, Co. Salop. The effigies of Sir Edward and his parents lie upon the Stanley Tomb at Tong Church, and the monument bears a verse in praise of the Stanleys, credibly attributed to Shakespeare; it concludes :-

"When all to Tyme's consumption shall be geaven,
"Standley for whom this stands shall stand in Heaven."

120
Figures, goats, sheep,
dog.
19¾in. × 36

Angels appearing to the Shepherds.
By Giacomo Bassano.

121

6in. high × 8½in. wide.

Jesus calling St. Peter out of the Boat.

By Breughel.

122

57in. × 58

The Saviour bearing the Cross.

By Paul Veronese.

123

Partly in armour. Red
slashed doublet, fair
hair; his hand rests
on a dog's head.

43½in. × 33

Sir Thomas Killigrew.

By Vandyck.

(1611—1683).

Younger son of Sir Robert Killigrew, of Hanworth, Co. Middlesex,
by Mary, daughter of Sir Thomas Wodehouse. He was Groom of the
Bedchamber to King Charles II., and his wit and humour made him
one of the favourites of the Court.

Bio. Cata. p. 148.

124

On panel.

18in. × 24½

A Battle.

By Cuyp.

125

Small Oval, on panel.

5in. × 7

Dœdalus and Icarus.

By Paul Brill.

126

Black dress, large lace
Elizabethan collar; red
feather in head-dress
and jewels.

20½in. × 17

Mistress Herbert.

By Zucchero.

(Died 1627).

She was mother of the statesman and philosopher Edward,
tenth Lord Herbert of Cherbury; Magdalen, fourth daughter of
Sir Richard Newport, by Margaret, daughter and heir of Sir Thomas
Bromley, one of the Executors of Henry VIII., having married, first,
Richard, grandson of Sir Richard Herbert, of Blackhall, Co. Montgomery, Kt.; and, secondly, Sir John Danvers, Kt., brother and heir
to Henry, Earl of Danby.

Bio. Cata. p. 153.

127

Shaven; looking
(in profile) to the left;
in black, and fur-trimmed
collar, chain, and George.

38in. × 51

Lord Cromwell.

By Holbein.

Thomas Cromwell, the son of a blacksmith at Putney, afterwards Earl of Essex. He filled many high offices of State to
Henry VIII. He succeeded Wolsey. The events of his life form an
important part of the annals of the reign of Henry VIII., and indeed,
of the Reformation. Executed on Tower Hill, 1540.

Bio. Cata. p. 155.

128

Pointer, Setter, Hare, &c.
20in. high × 15½in. wide

Dogs and Game, *By David de Koninck.*

129

White gown ; hands
crossed ; wreath on left
arm.
41in. × 32½

Lady Killigrew. *By Vandyck.*
Mistress Cecilia Crofts, Maid of Honour to Queen Henrietta
Maria.

130

17½in. × 27½

A Sea-piece, with Ships sailing. *By Vandervelde.*

131

Boats, tower, and
figures.
6in. × 8½

A View on the Rhine. *By Herman Sachtleven.*

132

Grasping a bow with a
broken string.
21in. × 27

Cupid reclining. *By Guido Reni.*

133

In pale yellow dress ;
leaning her elbow on a
table.
49½in. × 38¼

Grace, Countess of Dysart. *By Sir G. Kneller.*
(Died 1744.)
Eldest daughter and co-heiress of Sir Thomas Wilbraham,
by Elizabeth, daughter and heiress of Edward Mytton, Esq., of
Weston-under-Lizard. Married Lionel Tollemache, Earl of Dysart,
and, becoming co-heiress with the Countess of Bradford, carried large
estates to her husband's family.
Bio. Cata. p. 167

134

Pale yellow dress, pink
drapery ; holding a
flower.
49½in. × 38¼

Mary, Countess of Bradford. *By J. M. Wright.*
(1661—1737.)
Youngest daughter and co-heiress of Sir Thomas Wilbraham,
by Elizabeth, daughter and heiress of Edward Mytton, Esq., of
Weston-under-Lizard. Married Richard Newport, second Earl of
Bradford (*see No. 135*). Lady Bradford inherited the Weston estate,
and thus brought it to the Newport family. Born, married, and died
at Weston. Her two sons succeeded to the Earldom, viz.: Henry
and Thomas. Her daughters were, Mary, died unmarried ; Elizabeth,
married to James Cocks, Esq., of Worcester, ancestor to Lord Somers ;
Anne, co-heiress to the Weston Estates ; and Diana, who married
Algernon Coote, Earl of Montrath.
Bio. Cata. p. 168.

135

Slashed dress of golden
brown, white sleeves.
49in. high × 30in. wide.

Richard Newport, 2nd Earl of Bradford.

By Sir Peter Lely.

(1644—1728.)

Eldest son of the first Earl of Bradford, by Lady Diana Russell.
Married the daughter and co-heiress of Sir Thomas Wilbraham, of
Woodhey and Weston (*see No. 134.*)

Bio. Cata p. 169.

136

Oval in a square frame.
Holding the purse ; in the
robes of the Lord-Keeper.
28½in. × 24

Lord-Keeper Bridgeman.

By Sir Peter Lely

(1609—1674.)

The biography is given under the picture of Sir Orlando
Bridgeman, *No. 1* in this Catalogue—see pages 5 and 6.

137

In a black gown and ruff.
A shield bears the
episcopal arms of Chester
impaling Bridgeman.
22in. × 16

Doctor John Bridgeman, Bishop of Chester.

(1575—1657-8.)   *By C. Jansen.*

Father of the Lord Keeper. Grandson of Edward Bridgeman,
younger son of William Bridgeman, of Dean Magna, Co. Gloucester.
Married Elizabeth, daughter of Dr. Helyar (of a good old Somersetshire
family). Buried at Kinnerley, Salop. During the Civil War he had to
retire to his son's house at Morton, near Oswestry. Consecrated at
Lambeth, 1619. " He was the compiler of a valuable work relating to
" the Ecclesiastical Antiquities of the Diocese, now deposited in the
" Episcopal Registry, and usually denominated Bridgeman's Ledger."—

Ormerod's Cheshire.

Bio. Cata. p. 175.

138

Oval.
Blue coat, red overcoat.
27in. × 24

Sir Orlando Bridgeman, 4th Bart.   *By Vanderbank.*

(1695—1764.)

Son and successor of Sir John Bridgman, 3rd Bart., by Ursula
Matthews, of Blodwell. Married Lady Anne Newport, daughter and
heiress of Richard, 2nd Earl of Bradford.

Bio. Cata. p. 177.

139

Red coat ;
silver brandebourgs.
28in. × 22½

Henry Viscount Newport, afterwards Earl of Bradford.

By M. Dahl.

(Died 1784.)

Eldest son of Richard Newport, 2nd Earl, and Mary Wilbraham.
Represented Shropshire in several Parliaments, and was Lord Lieutenant
and Custos Rotulorum of the counties of Stafford, Salop, and Montgomery.
Unmarried. Buried in Henry VII.'s Chapel, at Westminster Abbey.
He alienated a large part of his property from his family.

Bio. Cata. p. 178.

140   Lady Anne Newport.   *By Vanderbank.*

White satin dress,
leaning her arm on a
table ; fair hair.
in. high × 24in. wide.

(1690—1752.)

Third daughter and co-heiress of Richard, second Earl of Bradford, and Mary Wilbraham. She married Sir Orlando Bridgeman, of Castle Bromwich, Bart. Besides having a large fortune, she brought the beautiful estate of Weston to the Bridgeman family. Her descendants are the only representatives of the Newport family.

Bio. Cata. p. 180.

141   Henry, 4th Lord Herbert of Cherbury.

By Wissing.

Oval.
in armour ; white lace
tie.
28in. × 22½

(died 1691.)

Son of Richard, second Lord Herbert of Cherbury, by Mary, daughter of John, Earl of Bridgewater. Married Lady Catherine Newport, daughter of Francis, first Earl of Bradford. His uncle Edward, first Lord Herbert of Cherbury, was the "noble author" of whom Horace Walpole speaks. His brother Edward, third Lord Herbert of Cherbury, the zealous loyalist, died without issue by either of his three wives, when the title and estates devolved upon Henry, fourth Lord, who also died without issue, when the title became extinct. His widow resided at Lymore, and, besides other charities, founded that noble charitable Institution called Preston Hospital, in Shropshire, built about 1727. She bequeathed £6,000 to purchase lands and to build thereon an almshouse for twelve women pensioners, and as a school for twelve girl boarders. Her brother, the Hon. Thomas Newport, created Lord Torrington, left his real estate at Preston for the same use, and £1,000 to build a hall in the middle of the almshouse. Her great nephew, Charles, last Earl of Mountrath, left £4,000 to supplement this Charity in 1802. New buildings have been added, and the number of women pensioners has been increased to twenty-seven, and the number of girls to twenty-five, the girls receiving an education especially fitting them for domestic service, and remaining in the Institution till the age of sixteen. Twenty of the pensioners now receive £32 a year, and seven £24 a year. Each has her separate domicile, and fuel free. The annuitants must be 60 years of age on entering, and be members of the Church of England. Lady Herbert directed that the Earl and Countess of Bradford should have the sole right of nominating beneficiaries of the Charity.

Bio. Cata. p. 181.

142

Oval, on the canvas.
Blue-grey cape with jewel
on shoulder ; orangy-brown
coat, grey sleeve.
27¼in. high × 24in. wide.

Sir John Bridgeman, 3rd Bart.

By Closterman.

(died 1747.)

Eldest son of Sir John Bridgeman, second Bart. Married Ursula, daughter and heiress of Roger Matthews, Esq., of Blodwell, Salop, a descendant of Madoc, last Prince of Powys.—*See No. 183.*

Bio. Cata. p. 187.

143

Oval.
In blue ; long fair wig.
28¼in. × 23

Francis, Earl of Bradford.

By M. Dahl.

(1619—1708.)

Francis Newport, second Lord Newport, first Earl of Bradford ; eldest son of Sir Richard Newport, of High Ercall, Kt. (created Lord Newport), who married Rachel, daughter of Sir John Leveson, and sister of Sir Richard Leveson, of Trentham, K.B. He married Lady Diana Russell, daughter of Francis, fourth Earl of Bedford.

Francis, Lord Newport, fought valiantly in the time of his father, under the Royal Banner, until 1644, when he was taken prisoner at Oswestry, and forced to compound for his estates by the payment of £5,284. He was one of the suspected lords whom Oliver Cromwell committed to the Tower. At the Restoration of Charles II. he was appointed Lord Lieutenant and Custos Rotulorum of Shropshire, and Controller and Treasurer of the Household, and a Privy Councillor. In 1675 he was created Viscount Newport. Soon after the accession of James II. he was superseded in consequence of his opposition to the arbitrary and unconstitutional measures of the new King ; he upheld the cause of religion at the trial of the seven Bishops, and voted for the succession of the Prince and Princess of Orange. On the day William III. and Mary II. were proclaimed, he was reinstated in his offices until he died at Twickenham. He was buried under a handsome monument at Wroxeter, Salop. King William paid him a visit and dined with him on his 80th birthday. He founded the almshouses at High Ercall, Salop. Of his large family, Richard succeeded him, and a younger son, Thomas, held various offices, and was created Baron Torrington, of Torrington, Co. Devon, having been thrice married.

Bio. Cata p. 183.

144

Pale yellow dress, grey
drapery ; pointing to
a tulip.
49in. × 39

Lady Wilbraham.

By Sir P. Lely.

(1631—1705.)

Elizabeth, daughter and sole heiress of Edward Mytton, of Weston, by Cecilia, daughter of Sir William Skeffington, of Fisherwick, Bart. She married Sir Thomas Wilbraham, Bart. She re-built the Church at Weston.—*Vide* the monumental inscription there.

Bio. Cata p. 186.

145 Sir Thomas Wilbraham, Bart. *By Verelst.*

Red coat, blue scarf.
59in. high × 38¼in. wide

Son of Sir Thomas Wilbraham, Bart., of Woodhey, by the daughter of Sir Roger Wilbraham. Married as above, and left three co-heiresses, viz :—Charlotte, wife of Sir Thomas Myddleton ; Mary, Countess of Bradford ; and Grace, Countess of Dysart. The direct male line of the ancient Cheshire family of Wilbraham ended with him.

Bio. Cata. p. 186.

146 Sir John Bridgeman, 2nd Bart. *By J. Vitors.*

Red dress, holding a jewelled sword.
30in. × 24¾

(1680—1710).

Eldest son of Sir Orlando Bridgeman, Lord Keeeper. Married Mary, daughter and heiress of George Cradock, Esq., of Carsewell, (Caverswall) Castle, whose widow married Sir Orlando as his second wife.

Bio. Cata. p 182.

147 Sir Henry Bridgeman and Family. *By Pine.*

Sir Henry in yellow hat and feathers. Lady B. in red. Eldest daughter in pink, playing a harpsichord ; sister in white, playing a harp ; Orlando in red ; John in blue ; George seated.
81in. × 101

Sir Henry Bridgeman, first Baron Bradford, (1725—1800), eldest surviving son of Sir Orlando and Lady Anne. Lady Bradford, (1735-1806), daughter and heiress of the Rev. John Simpson, of Stoke Hall. The elder daughter married Henry Greswold Lewis, Esq., of Malvern Hall. The younger daughter married Sir George W. Gunning, Bart. Sir Henry inherited the Weston Estates on the death of Thomas Newport, last Earl of Bradford, in 1762. Sir Henry sat in Parliament for many years, and in 1794 was advanced to the peerage as Baron Bradford, of Bradford, Co. Salop. Orlando, his son and successor, was second Baron, and first Earl of Bradford. John, of Babworth, assumed the name and arms of Simpson, and married the heiress of Sir Thomas Worsley, of Appuldercombe, Bart. George became Rector of Wigan and Weston ; married first, Lady Lucy Boyle, and secondly, Charlotte Louisa Poyntz.

Bio. Cata. p. 188.

148 The Hon. Mrs. Gunning. *By Hoppner.*

White lace cap and fichu.
29¼in. × 24½

(1764—1810).

Elizabeth, second daughter of Henry Lord Bradford. Married George Gunning, Esq., afterwards a Baronet, of Horton, County Northampton.

Bio. Cata. p. 189.

149

Black dress and cap, shield of arms in right hand corner.
22in. high × 17in. wide.

Mrs. Bridgeman.

By C. Jansen.

(died 1636).

She married John Bridgeman, Bishop of Chester. Daughter of Dr. Helyar, Canon of Exeter and Archdeacon of Barnstaple. Buried in Chester Cathedral.

Bio. Cata. p. 189.

150

77in. × 52½

A Woman bathing.

By Simon Voët.

151

Oval.
Black coat, blue overcoat on left arm; long black wig.
28in. × 24

Orlando Bridgeman, Esq.

By M. Dahl.

(1671—1721).

Fifth son of Sir John Bridgeman, 2nd Baronet, M.P. for Wigan 1698-1702. Married Catherine, daughter of William Bridgeman, Esq., of Combes, Secretary to the Admiralty.

Bio. Cata. p. 190.

152

Oval.
As a child; white frock; with an Italian grey-hound.
28in. × 24

Miss Bridgeman, afterwards the Hon. Mrs. Greswold Lewis.

(1761—1802).

Charlotte, elder daughter of Henry Lord Bradford. Married Henry Greswold Lewis, Esq., of Malvern Hall, Co. Warwick. Buried at Yardley, Co. Worcester.

Bio. Cata. p. 190.

153

Oval on the canvas.
Brown gown, black mob cap.
28in. × 28½

Lucy, Viscountess Torrington.

By Gainsborough.

(1744—1792).

Daughter of John Boyle, Earl of Cork and Orrery. Married George, 4th Viscount Torrington, and left four daughters—Lady John Russell; Lucy, Countess of Bradford; the Marchioness of Bath, and Emily, who married Henry, eldest son of Lord Robert Seymour.

Bio. Cata. p. 191.

154

Brown dress, long lace
collar, loose white cuffs,
wig.
!1⅜in. high × ⅔4in. wide

Lionel Tollemache, 2nd Earl of Dysart.

(1648—1727.)

Son of Sir Lionel Tollemache, of Helmingham. He succeeded his mother, Countess of Dysart, in her own right, daughter and heiress of the first Earl. He married Grace, daughter and co-heiress of Sir Thomas and Lady Wilbraham, and left a son and two daughters.

Bio. Cata. p. 191.

155

Pink and blue;
mask brooch.
20⅛in. × 17¼

Portrait of a young Lady.

By Mrs. Beale.

156

Half length, in white;
lace tie, jewels, and
yellow rose; lace
head-dress.
24in. × 20

The Countess of Bradford

By Clifford.

(1819—1894.)

Selina Louisa, the youngest daughter of the 1st Lord Forester and Lady Katherine Manners, daughter of Charles, Duke of Rutland. She married, in 1844, Orlando George Charles, 3rd Earl of Bradford. Their Golden Wedding was celebrated April the 30th, 1894, and on November 25th of the same year Lady Bradford passed away to rest. The Almshouses at Weston, for four poor women, were founded by her in 1874. Of Lady Bradford's six children, four survive, viz.; George Cecil Orlando (Viscount Newport), Col. the Hon. Francis Charles Bridgeman, Lady Mabel Kenyon-Slaney, and the Countess of Harewood.

157

Within an oval, on the
canvas.
Long hair, pale coat,
orange brown scarf.
29½in. × 24¾

Portrait of a Mr. Bridgeman, of Devonshire.

(This picture was given to the Earl of Bradford by the Hon. and Rev. Henry Bridgeman; as also No. 160.)

158

Blue cap and white
feather, lace stomacher
and sleeves.
21in. × 17½

Miss Diana Bridgeman.

By F. Cotes.

(1726—1764.)

Daughter of Sir Orlando and Lady Anne Bridgeman. Married John Sawbridge, Esq., of Olantigh, Kent. Buried at Wye, Co. Kent.

Bio. Cata. p. 243.

159

Blue dress ; pointing
with her right hand.
39in. high x 33in. wide.

Charlotte, Countess of Warwick, and afterwards Wife of Mr. Addison.

By Sir Godfrey Kneller.

Daughter of Sir Thomas Myddleton, Bart., by Charlotte, only surviving daughter of the Lord-Keeper Bridgeman. Miss Myddleton married, first, Edward, Earl of Warwick and Holland, and, secondly, the Right Hon. Joseph Addison.

(This picture was exhibited at the National Portrait Exhibition,
South Kensington. in 1867.)
Bio. Cata. p. 244.

160

Within an oval on the
canvas.
Yellow-brown satin ; red
scarf, jewelled cord.
. 29¼in. × 24½

Portrait of a Mrs. Bridgeman, of Devonshire.

Wife of No. 157.

161

In blue, with a Spaniel.
21in. × 17½ '

.

Lady Mary Newport.

By Mrs. Beale.

Died in 1711, unmarried, aged 30. Daughter of Richard, second Earl of Bradford, and sister of Henry and Thomas, 3rd and 4th Earls, of the Newport family.

162

In green, trimmed with
ermine ; muff, necklace,
and throat band.
29in. × 24

Elizabeth, Lady Bradford.

By Pine.

Wife of Henry, 1st Baron Bradford, daughter of the Rev. John Simpson, of Stoke Hall, Co. Derby (*see No. 147*).

163

Horse, dogs, man, and
goat.
37½in. × 51½

Landscape, with a Pack-Horse

By Rosa da Tivoli.

164

37½in. × 51¼

Landscape, with a Shower of Rain.

By Lankrink.

165

Mary, Queen of Scots.

Hall length. Red dress, embroidered ; pearls and cross ; jewels in her hair.
29¼in.high × 24½in.wide

(1542—1587.)

Daughter of James V. of Scotland, and Mary of Lorraine. Succeeded her father before she was a week old. Married, (1) The Dauphin of France, 1558 ; (2) Lord Darnley, 1565 ; (3) the Earl of Bothwell, 1567. She claimed the Throne of England on the ground of Queen Elizabeth's illegitimacy, and was imprisoned from 1568 until her execution in 1587.

(This picture belonged to Mrs. Bedford, sister of Mrs. Kirkpatrick Sharpe, of Hoddam Castle.)

" This is supposed to be a copy from an original by *Zucchero*, now lost; there are copies at the Marquess of Ailsa's, and some other Scottish houses, similar to this."—*Letter from the Rev. W. Bedford.*

166

Mrs. Davis. *By Sir Peter Lely.*

Seated playing a guitar, old yellow-brown satin gown.
48in. × 39½

Mistress Mary, or Moll Davis, was an actress, and favourite of Charles II., by whom she had, in 1673, a daughter, Mary Tudor, who married Francis Ratcliffe, afterwards 2nd Earl of Derwentwater, who died in 1705.

Bio. Cata. p. 245.

167

Allegorical—(Plenty ?) *By Amiconi.*

Nude winged figure, holding wreath of corn, roses, &c.
42½in. × 37½

Perhaps cut out of a picture.

168

Portrait of a Lady. *By Sir Antonio More.*

White cap, black dress, chain girdle.
24¼in. × 20¾

169

Allegorical—(Peace ?) *By Amiconi.*

Crouching youth clasping a lion ; spray of barley, &c.
42½in. × 37½

Perhaps cut out of a picture.

170

The continence of Scipio. *By Simon de Vos.*

27in. × 38

171

Oval.
Round black hat and coat,
brown vest cut square,
chain, and medallion ;
right hand holds a roll.
14½in.high × 11¼in wide

Portrait of a Gentleman.

By Philip de Koning.

172

81in. × 88

Jacob at the Well.

By Francesco Bassano.

173

As a youth. Light coloured
sleeves and cloak, white
under sleeves, lace collar
and tassels, long hair.
24in. × 20

Orlando Bridgeman, 2nd Baron, and 1st Earl of Bradford.

By Pine.

(1762—1825.)

Second, but eldest surviving son of Henry, Lord Bradford. He was M.P. for Wigan in 1784, 1790, and 1796. Created Viscount Newport and Earl of Bradford in Co. Salop, November 30th, 1815. He married, in 1788, Lucy Elizabeth, daughter and co-heiress of George, 4th Viscount Torrington.

Bio. Cata. p. 249.

174

As a boy. Buff coat,
white collar.
16½in. × 15

George Byng, 4th Viscount Torrington.

By Ramsay.

(Died 1812.) Elder son of the third Viscount and Elizabeth, granddaughter of Sir Peter Daniel, Kt. Married, in 1765, Lady Lucy Boyle, only daughter of John, Earl of Cork and Orrery, by whom he had four surviving daughters, viz.: Lucy, Countess of Bradford ; Georgina, wife of Lord John Russell, afterwards Duke of Bedford ; Isabella, Marchioness of Bath ; and Emily, who married Henry, eldest son of Lord Robert Seymour.

Bio. Cata. p. 249.

175

Claret coat ; powder.
17in. × 17½

Sir Orlando Bridgeman, 4th Bart.

By F. Cotes.

(1695—1764.)

M.P. for Shrewsbury, 1722. Married Lady Anne Newport.

(*See No. 140.*)

176

Oval.
Purple and white dress ;
green and red bow on left
shoulder, pearl necklet.
20½in. × 17½

Nell Gwynne.

By Mrs. Beale.

(Died 1687.)

She at first sold oranges in taverns and theatres, then went on the stage, and became a favourite of Charles II., and was mother (by him) of the Duke of St. Albans. She once gave the King advice how to please the people, viz. : " Dismiss your ladies, and attend to your business."

Bio. Cata. p. 250.

177
45in high. × 45¼ wide

A Council of War.

By Leandro Bassano.

In the Newport Catalogue.

178
In a blue dress.
20¼in. × 17½

Portrait of a Lady.

By G. Murphy.

179
41in. × 66½in.

Sleeping Venus.

After Titian.

180
21in. × 17.

The Spoils of War.

181
27½in. × 37½

Two Boys playing.

By Vandyck.

182
Red dress, lace cravat,
short white wig.
27in. × 22½

Portrait of a Gentleman.

183
Low brown dress, white
sleeves, pearls in her hair,
nursing a little dog.
(See No. 523.)
29½in. × 24½

Portrait of a Lady, supposed to be Ursula,
wife of Sir John Bridgeman, 3rd Bart.
(1671—1719).

She was daughter and sole heir of Roger Matthews, Esq., of
Blodwell, Co. Salop, representative of John Matthews, Esq., of Court,
and Jane his wife, elder daughter and co-heir of Morris Tanat, Esq.,
of Blodwell, derived from Einion Efell, Lord of Cynllaeth, a son
of Madoc, last Prince of Powys. This marriage added many quarterings
to the Bridgeman Shield of Arms.

184
25in. × 36½

A Landscape, "Langdale."

185
43in. × 55

A large Dog, (which belonged to Orlando, Lord Bradford),
with *Jacobe*, a German Servant. *By Weaver.*

186
25in. × 36¼

A Landscape, "Honister Crag."

187

Brown dress, long hair,
lace cravat.

27¼in.high × 21¼in.wide

Francis, 2nd Baron Newport, afterwards Earl of Bradford. *By Sir Godfrey Kueller.*

(1619—1708).

Biography, *see under No. 143, †, 23.*

188

Hunting dress, a
fox's brush upon table.

29½in. × 24½

George Forester, Esq., of Willey.

(1762—1811).

Son of Brook Forester, Esq., and Elizabeth, daughter and heir of George Weld, Esq., of Willey Park, Co. Salop. His cousin succeeded to his estates, viz :—Cecil Weld Forester created Baron Forester 1821, the father of Selina Louisa, Countess of Bradford.

Bio. Cata. p. 253.

189

Red dress, lace cravat,
short white wig.

29½in. × 24½

Portrait of a Gentleman.

190

In cap and gown. On a
shield the
Arms of the See of Chester
impaling Bridgeman.

29½in. × 24½

John Bridgeman, Bishop of Chester. *By Van Somers.*

(1577—1652).

Father of the Lord Keeper. Grandson of Edward Bridgeman, High Sheriff 1578 of the city and County of Exeter; M.A. 1600; attained at Oxford Doctor of Divinity, the highest degree a "scholar can receive or the University bestow." Dr. Bridgeman's character for learning and piety, combined with his refinement of manners and good breeding, had reached the ears of King James I, who appointed him one of his domestic Chaplains in 1605. Soon after he became incumbent of Wigan ; 1619 raised to the See of Chester, and His Majesty gave him the living of Bangor *ad commendam*. He was absent from the Upper House in 1641, when the Bishops protested against the proceedings of Parliament, and were impeached and sent to the Tower, But all his proclivities were Royalist, and during the Usurpation, his estates being sequestrated, he took refuge at his son's (the Lord Keeper's) country house, at Morton, near Oswestry, Salop, where he died in 1652, being buried in the neighbouring church of Kinnerley, where there is a momument to his memory. At Chester Cathedral still remains the curious Consistory Court with fittings bearing the Bishop's Arms, and in the north aisle is the Bishop's pew. He married Elizabeth, daughter of the Ven. Archdeacon Helyar, his eldest surviving son being Orlando, the Lord Keeper.

His second son Dove, was Prebendary of Chester, whose widow surviving, re-married Dr. Hackett, Bishop of Lichfield. The third son,

Henry, became Rector of Bangor and Barrow, Dean of Chester, and Bishop of Sodor and Man 1671. He died in 1682, having married, first, Catherine, daughter of William Lever, of Kersall, Lancashire, Gent.; and their daughter, Elizabeth, married Sir Thomas Greenhalgh. The fourth son, Sir James Bridgeman, Kt., left two daughters—Frances, married to William, third Lord Howard of Escrick, and Magdalen, wife of William Wynde, Esq. The fifth son was Richard, a merchant of Amsterdam. There were ten other children, who died young.

"Bishop Bridgeman was the compiler of a valuable work relating to the Ecclesiastical Antiquities of the Diocese, now deposited in the Episcopal Registry, and usually denominated 'Bridgeman's Ledger.' "— *Ormerod's Cheshire.*

Bio. Cata. p. 175, and see No. 137.

191

Cuirass. White sleeves, embroidered in gold; lace collar, belt over right, and ribbon over left shoulder.

30in. high × 24¾in. wide

Henry Rich, Earl of Holland, K.G.   *By Henry Stone.*

Executed 1649. Second son of Robert Rich, first Earl of Warwick, by Lady Penelope Devereux, daughter of Walter, Earl of Essex. Married the rich heiress of Sir John Cope, of Kensington. Created Earl of Holland. Cromwell, it would appear, disliked him extremely, and accordingly Lord Holland suffered death immediately after the Duke of Hamilton.

His son succeeded him as Earl of Holland, and became Earl of Warwick on the death of his uncle, 1672.

Bio. Cata. p. 195.

192

Oval.
Blue dress, long wig.
30in. × 24

Francis Newport, 1st Earl of Bradford.

After Dahl.

Died 1708, aged 88.

See Nos. 143 and 187, and in Bio. Cata. pp. 183 and 197.

193

In armour, brown dress.
26¼in. × 22

Marshal Turenne.

(1611—1675.) Killed in action.

Henri de la Tour d'Auvergne, second son of the Duke de Bouillon, and Elizabeth, of Nassau, daughter of William the Silent. "His military exploits, his daring gallantry and skill as a commander have made his name world-renowned, and the battles that he won, the wonderful vicissitudes of his career, both political and military, belong to the pages of European history."

Turenne was presented to Philip IV. of Spain, who said, after gazing on him in silence for some minutes, "so this is the man who has made me to pass so many a sleepless night." He married Mademoiselle de Caumont, only daughter of the Duke de la Force.

Bio. Cata. p. 197.

196

In green and blue ; curls,
pearl earrings and necklet ;
a mole on her chin.

29¼in.high × 24¾in.wide

Lady Porter.

By Hale.

(In Torrington Catalogue of 1719.)

197

30in. × 48

Three Dogs.

By G. W. Horlor, 1866.

198

In pale grey and green,
holding a nosegay, leaning
on a balustrade. Green
bow, red curtains.

48¾in. × 39¼

Lady Myddleton.

Charlotte, Lady Myddleton, daughter of Lord-Keeper Bridgeman,
married Sir Thomas Myddleton, of Chirk, Co. Denbigh, Bart. Her
daughter married, first, Edward, Earl of Warwick, and, secondly, the
Right Hon. Joseph Addison.

199

Brown coat, fur collar,
white neck cloth.

35½in. × 27¼

George Augustus Frederick Henry, Viscount Newport, afterwards 2nd Earl of Bradford.

(1789 - 1856.)   *By Sir Geo. Hayter, R.A., 1819.*

Eldest son of Orlando Bridgeman, first Earl, and the Hon. Lucy
Byng. Married Georgina Elizabeth, only daughter of Sir Thomas
Moncreiffe, Bart., of Montcreiffe, by whom he had Orlando George, his
successor, the present Earl; the Hon. and Rev. George Bridgeman,
Rector of Wigan, Hon. Chaplain to Her Majesty, and Hon. Canon of
Chester; the Hon. and Rev. John R. O. Bridgeman, Rector of Weston;
and five daughters, of whom Elizabeth Lucy died young ; Georgina
Elizabeth, (died in 1843, and who, with her mother, form the subject of
an elegant group of marble to their memory in Weston Church) ; Lucy
Caroline, and Charlotte Anne, who both died from the awful effects of
fire in 1858 ; and Mary Selina Louisa, who married the Hon. Robert
Windsor Clive, eldest son of the Hon. Robert Henry Clive and Harriet,
Baroness Windsor. The Earl married, secondly, Helen, widow of Sir
David Moncreiffe, Bart., and daughter of Æneas Makay, Esq., of Scotston,
Peebles. She died in 1869.

Bio. Cata. p. 202.

200

Black coat, ribbon, Order of the Thistle, and Star.

29½in. high × 24in. wide

The Marquess of Dalhousie.

By G. F. Clark, after Sir J. Watson-Gordon.

(1812—1860.)

James Andrew Ramsay, eldest surviving son of the ninth Earl of Dalhousie. Was Governor-General of India, and created a Marquess for his eminent services in 1849. On his death the Marquessate became extinct. Married Lady Susan Georgina, daughter of George, Marquess of Tweeddale.

201

Full length.
In black velvet; boots and spurs, riding whip, retriever at his feet.

87in. × 51

Orlando George Charles, 3rd Earl of Bradford.

(Born April 24, 1819.)   *By Sir Francis Grant.*

Eldest son of the second Earl of Bradford and Georgina, only daughter of Sir Thomas Moncreiffe, Bart. Educated at Harrow and at Trinity College, Cambridge; was M.P. for Shropshire from 1842 until he succeeded to the Earldom in 1865; was Vice-Chamberlain of the Royal Household from February till December, 1852, and from February, 1858, till June, 1859; Lord Chamberlain from 1866 till December, 1868; and Master of the Horse to the Queen from 1874 till 1880, and again from June, 1885, till February, 1886; Deputy-Lieutenant for Staffordshire and Warwickshire; Captain of the Salopian Yeomanry, 1844, and Lieut.-Col. of the 1st. Batt. Shropshire Volunteers; Lord-Lieutenant and Custos Rotulorum of Shropshire since 1875.—*(See No. 83.)*

206

Oval.
Dark cloak, white neck cloth.

29¼in. × 24½

The Duke of Wellington.

{ *The head is by Hayter.*
{ *Completed by Wm. Proctor.*

(1769—1852.)

The Iron Duke, Warrior, Patriot, Statesman.

" His biography belongs to the annals of his country."—*Miss Boyle.*

208

10in. × 24¾

Noah entering into the Ark.

By Hondt.

209

12¼in. × 19½

The Martyrdom of St. Sebastian.

By Jacques Callot.

40

210
Black gown, small dog
in her lap.

The Hon. Selina Louisa Forester, afterwards
Countess of Bradford. *By Sir Francis Grant, P.R.A.*

(See No. 156.)

211
6in. high × 8in. wide.

Fruit. *By De Heem.*

212
19in. × 24¾

The Creation. *By Hondt.*

213
9¾in. × 14½

A lean white Horse. *By Peter de Laer*

(" A Lean Horse, by Bamboots."—Newport Catalogue.)

214
In Crayons.
Red habit, blue waistcoat,
with a little dog beside
her.
20in. × 16

Elizabeth, Lady Bradford.

Daughter and sole heiress of the Rev. John Simpson, of Stoke
Hall, Co. Derby. Married in 1755 Sir Henry Bridgeman, Baron
Bradford. Her second surviving son, John Bridgeman, of Babworth,
Notts, assumed the name and arms of Simpson in 1785, founding the
Bridgeman-Simpson family.

(See Nos. 147 and 162.)

215
In Crayons.
Blue coat, holding hat in
right hand. Dog.
20in. × 16

Henry, Lord Bradford.

Only son of Sir Orlando Bridgeman and Lady Anne Newport.
Born 1725, died 1800.

(See No. 147.)

216
18in. × 14½

China. *By Roestraeten.*

217
14¼in. × 11

Female Figures, with Skull and Cupid.

After Domenichino.

218

In Oriental costume.
24in. high × 20½in. wide

Hamet Ben Hamet.

By Sir G. Kneller.

("Ye Russhia Ambassador," *1719 Catalogue.*)

(Ambassador from the King of Morocco to Charles II.—*1837 catalogue.*)

219

14in. × 9½

Virgin and Child.

School of Correggio.

220

Half length.
Black dress, white cap.

H.M. Queen Victoria.

By J. Blake Wirgman, 1877.

Painted at Osborne.

221

18in. × 14½

Parrot and Flowers.

By Verelst.

("A piece of Flowers and a Parrot," *1719 Catalogue.*)

223

Black coat, white waist-
coat. Order of the Golden
Fleece : Ribbon of the
Garter.
23½in. × 19¼

The Duke of Wellington.

By Sir Geo. Hayter.

(See No. 206.)

224

15½in. × 12¾

Fruit.

By De Heem.

225

Old woman in a white
cap looking out of an
oval stone window.
16½in. × 14½

Mary Yates.

By Colombo.

(Died 1776, aged 127 years.)

She holds a board, on which is inscribed "Mary Yates, aged 127 years. Born at Wheaton Aston, in Staffordshire. She enjoyed her senses till her death, but she was helpless five years before she died, which was in August, 1776. G.B.I."

226

Blue dress, little dog
at her feet.
14in. × 10

The Countess of Kingston.

By Mrs. Beale.

Anne, daughter of Robert, fourth Lord Brooke, and wife of William Pierpoint, fourth Earl of Kingston, uncle to Lady Mary Wortley Montague, celebrated in the literary world.

229
Crayons.
A head. She wears a
bonnet : hair in curls.
9½in. high × 7¾in. wide.

Lucy Elizabeth, Dowager Countess of Bradford.

By Sir Wm. Ross.

(Born 1766, died 1844.)

Daughter and co-heiress of George, fourth Viscount Torrington, and Lady Lucy Boyle. She married in 1788 Orlando, afterwards first Earl of Bradford.

230
Black dress, holding
a roll.
16in. × 13½

Lord John Russell.

By Sir G. Hayter.

(1792—1878.)

The eminent Statesman and Author. Youngest son of Lord John Russell, afterwards sixth Duke of Bedford, and the Hon. Georgina Elizabeth Byng. His journey to the Peninsula, in company with Lord Bradford and Mr. Robert Clive, had the happy effect of modifying his early French ideas, which were ardently in favour of the French Revolution. An interesting account of this journey is found in the "Letters from Portugal, Spain, Sicily, and Malta, in 1812, 1813, and 1814, by G.A.F.H.B.," published in 1875 by the Earl of Bradford.

231
Crayons.
Black gown.
10in. × 8

The Hon. Henry Edmund Bridgeman.

By Shartles.

(1795—1872.)

Sometime Rector of Blymhill, Staffordshire. He afterwards embraced the Irvingite doctrine. Son of the first Earl of Bradford. Married his cousin, Louisa Elizabeth, daughter of the Hon. John Bridgeman Simpson.

232
Oval.
High white dress and blue
sash. Powder.
Large hat.
9¼in. × 7½

The Hon. Mrs. Bridgeman Simpson.

(1758—1791.)

Henrietta Frances, only daughter of Sir Thomas Worsley, of Appuldercombe, Isle of Wight, Bart. Married in 1784 the Hon. John Bridgeman (second surviving son of Henry, first Baron Bradford), who assumed the name and arms of Simpson, by Act of Parliament, 1785. Their son William died at School, 1794 ; and their daughter Henrietta inherited the estates of her uncle, Sir Richard Worsley, and married Charles, first Earl of Yarborough.

Bio. Cata. p. 209.

233

Two children seated;
the girl's arm round her
brother's neck, holding
flowers.
19¼in.high × 15¼in.wide

Sir Thomas Moncreiffe, Bart., and his sister Helen, afterwards Mrs. Wright, of Halston.

By Sir William Ross.

He was seventh Bart. Born 1822, died 1879. She married Edmnnd Wright, Esq., of Halston, Co. Salop, and died in 1874.

234

In Pastel.
An old gentleman, with stick
and book. Wears his hat.
10in. × 8½

The Rev. Leonard Chappelow. *By Sharples.*

Chaplain to Henry, first Lord Bradford.

235

Oval. In Pastel.
Blue coat, buff waistcoat.
9in. × 7½

Orlando Bridgeman, Esq., afterwards 1st Earl of Bradford.

Son of Henry, first Baron Bradford.

(See No. 68.)

236

Seated : black coat,
white waistcoat, right
hand in his bosom.
14in. × 11½

Orlando Bridgeman, Esq., afterwards 1st Earl of Bradford.

Painted in 1822. *(See No. 68.)*

237

In red : hands clasped,
leaning on a table.
18in. × 15

A Madonna. *Venetian School.*

238

8½in. × 11½

The Saviour betrayed by Judas. *By Guercino.*

239

27in. × 84

A Landscape and Figures. *By Peter Breydel.*

("A Dutch Landscape, with figures, bv *Bredael.*")—*Torrington Catalogue.*

240

Circular.
17in. diameter.

A Landscape. *By Old Breughel.*

241

27in. high × 88½in. wide

A Landscape and Figures.   By *Peter Breydel.*

(In the Torrington Catalogue.)

242

On Copper.
14in. × 11½

The Crown of Thorns.

243

10in. × 12

Landscape.   By *Peter de Laer.*

244

Mauve dress, cut square ;
head-dress of mauve ribbon
and white feathers,
necklace and earrings.
25in. × 20½

Maria Christina, Archduchess of Austria, Regent of the Netherlands.

Maria Christina, of Austria, sister of the Emperor Joseph II., was named Gouvèrnante des Pays Bas, conjointly with her husband, Albert Casimer, Duke of Saxe-Teschen, in 1781. They made their entry into Brussels 10th July the same year.

(Biographical Catalogue, page 214, called " A Princess of Bavaria.")

245

10in. × 13½

Jesus casting out Devils.   By *Paul Brill.*

(1719 Catalogue.)

246

18in. × 14½

St. Catherine, Virgin and Martyr.

After Domenichino.

247

In Chalk;
24in. × 19½

Orlando G. C., Viscount Newport.

By *James Swinton.*

Bio. Cata. p. 216.

248

In Chalk.
Torquoise necklace.
24in. × 19½

Selina Louisa, Viscountess Newport.

By *James Swinton.*

Bio. Cata. p. 216.

249
7¼in. high × 10½in. wide

Glaucus and Scylla.
By Filippo Lauri.

("A Nymph and a Triton," *by Ph. Lauri.*)—*1719 Catalogue.*

250
18in. × 20

A Supper.
By Cornelius de Waal.

251
In an evening dress, pale
blue and red; tiara, necklace,
and earrings. Red ribbon,
gold jewelled chain.
23½in. × 19¼

H.M. Queen Victoria.
By Clarke, after Winterhalter.
Bio. Cata. p. 217.

252
10in. × 16

Entering into the Ark.
By Ben. Castiglione.

("Noah's Ark," in the *Newport Catalogue.*)

253
23in. × 18

Fruit and Flowers.
By Campidoglio.

254
18in. × 15

Allegorical.
School of Rubens.

255
18in. × 15½

Allegorical.
School of Rubens.

256
10¼in. × 10¾

A Landscape.
School of Rembrandt.

257
23in. × 18

Flowers and Fruit.
By Campidoglio.

258
22in. × 29

Diana and her Nymphs.
School of Rubens.

46

259
18in. high × 16in. wide.

Six subjects from Holy Scripture. *By Pietro Perugino.*

262
85½in. × 50

Elizabeth, Lady Bradford.
(See Nos. 147 and 214.)

265
Crayon.
10¾in. × 8

Rembrandt.

266
Crayon.
12¼in. × 9

Rubens.

267
Crayon.
11½in. × 9

Butler (Author of "Hudibras").

268
Oval. A Crayon.
10¼in. × 8½

4th Viscount Torrington. *By A. D. Hamilton, 1772.*

269
A Water Colour.
24½in. × 17¼

Sir David Moncreiffe, Bart.

270
As a boy.
9¾in. × 8¼

Mr. George Bridgeman, afterwards 2nd Earl of Bradford.
(1799.)

271
Oval.
10½in. × 8¼

The Hon. Lucy Byng, afterwards Countess of Bradford.

272
Small bed in background.
5¼in. × 6¾

An Interior, with Figures.

274
4in. × 3¼

The Martyrdom of St. Lawrence.

278

Crayon.

13in. high × 10¾in. wide

The Rev. W. Bates, of Willey.

290

A Landscape.   *By Charles, 6th Duke of Rutland.*

293
294

12in. × 8½

12in. × 8½

Lord Londesborough and Lady Londesborough,

(1805—1860.)   (1823—1883.)

his second wife.

Sketches in Oil, by F. Grant.

Lord Albert Conyngham, second surviving son of Henry, first Marquis Conyngham, and Elizabeth, daughter of Joseph Denison, Esq., of Denbies, Co. Surrey, succeeded to the large estates and fortunes of his maternal uncle, and assumed the surname and arms of Denison, being elevated to the Peerage as Baron Londesborough.

Lady Londesborough, his second wife, was Ursula, eldest daughter of Admiral the Hon. Charles Bridgeman, of Knockin Hall.

Lord Londesborough's first wife was the Hon. Henrietta Maria Forester (sister of the Countess of Bradford), who died in 1841.

Bio. Cata. p. 231.

313

The Earl of Bradford—Leicestershire scene.

By Ferneley, 1866,

322

15½in. × 19½

The Ladies Sarah and Clementina Villiers.

By Chalon.

Daughters of the fifth Earl of Jersey and Lady Sarah Fane, daughter of the tenth Earl of Westmoreland.

329

Lady Mabel Bridgeman.   *By E. Clifford.*

Mabel Selina, elder daughter of Orlando George Charles, third Earl of Bradford.   *(See No. 387.)*

330

14in. × 19¼

Hon. George C. O. Bridgeman.

(1846.)   *(See No. 304.)*

343

17¼in. high × 23in. wide

Castle Bromwich Hall, from the Avenue.

By A. Everitt.

344

Water Colour.

17½in. × 22

Landscape, with Cattle and Sheep.   *By Cooper.*

346

18in. × 24¾

The Earl of Bradford and F. Gillard, and the Belvoir Hounds; the Duke of Rutland in the distance.   *By F. Grant.*

347

21¼in. × 26½

Lichfield Cathedral.   *By Fernyhough.*

This view is taken from near the willow tree planted by Dr. Johnson. (The picture was once in the possession of Miss Anna Seward.)

354

Oval.

21in. × 17¼

Lady Albert Conyngham.   *By F. Grant.*

(1809—1841.)

The Hon. Henrietta Maria, fourth daughter of the first Lord Forester; married, in 1833, Lord Albert Conyngham, afterwards known as Lord Albert Denison, K.C.H., F.S.A., and created Lord Londesborough.

355

16½in. × 25¼

Her Majesty Queen Victoria.   *By G. Thomas.*

Investing the Sultan with the Order of the Garter, on board the Royal Yacht. Painted, by permission of Her Majesty, for Lord Bradford, who was Lord Chamberlain, and assisted at the ceremony.

356

19¾in. × 27½

Head of Windermere.   *By Glover.*

357

17½in. × 22

Sea Sketch.   *By Copley Fielding.*

358
9in. high × 7in. wide.

Italian Children.   *By G. Fortunati.*

378
20in. × 18

The Queen in St. George's Chapel, Windsor, at the Marriage of the Prince of Wales, 1863.   *By Thomas.*
(Original Sketch.)

382
Oval.
8in. × 5¾

Landscape.   *By Claude Lorraine.*

383
7½in. × 6¼

Virgin and Child.   *Italian.*

387
29in. × 21¼

The Hon. Mabel and Hon. Florence Bridgeman.
By A. Blackley, 1862.

The elder daughter of Orlando George Charles, third Earl of Bradford, Mabel Selina. Born 13th November, 1855; married, February 22nd, 1887, Colonel William Slaney Kenyon-Slaney, of Hatton Grange, Co. Salop, born 1847, J.P., M.P. for the Newport Division of Shropshire since 1886, and has issue, Sybil Agnes, born January 26th, 1888; Robert Orlando Rodolph, born January 15th, 1892. Colonel Kenyon-Slaney is the eldest son of Colonel William Kenyon (Grandson of Lord Chief-Justice Kenyon) and Fanny Catherine, third daughter and co-heir of Robert Aglionby Slaney, Esq., of Walford Manor and Hatton Grange, Shropshire, M.P. for Shrewsbury.

Florence Katherine, younger daughter, born 12th February, 1859, married, 5th November, 1881, Henry Ulick, Viscount Lascelles (now Earl of Harewood), and has issue, Hon. Henry George Charles (now Viscount Lascelles), born 9th September, 1882; Hon. Edward Cecil, born July, 1887; and Lady Margaret Selina, born 11th August, 1883.

390
Full length. As a boy.
37½in. × 25

Hon. Gerald O. M. Bridgeman.   *By Lundgren.*
(See No. 304.)

391

15½in.high × 10¾in.wide

Anne Elizabeth, Countess of Chesterfield.

By Miss Cruickshank, after Sir E. Landseer.

(1802—1885.)

Eldest daughter of Cecil, first Lord Forester, and Lady Katherine Mary Manners, second daughter of Charles, fourth Duke of Rutland. She was the eldest sister of the Countess of Bradford, and married George Stanhope, sixth Earl of Chesterfield, and had issue, George, seventh Earl, and Evelyn, who married Henry, fourth Earl of Carnarvon.

393

Drawing.

5in. × 7¼

Scene from the Life of Bishop Bridgeman.

By Cattermole.

493

9½in. × 8

Hon. Orlando and Hon. Henry Bridgeman, as Cherubs, 1798.

Sons of Orlando, first Earl of Bradford. Orlando, born 1794, died at Hastings, 1827. Married Lady Selina daughter of the first Earl of Kilmorey.

Henry Edmund, born 1795, sometime Rector of Blymhill. Died in 1872, having married Louisa, daughter of the Hon. John Bridgeman Simpson, of Babworth.

494

14in. × 10½

Viscount Newport, 1840.

496

4in. × 4

Lady Charlotte, Lady Mary, and the Hon. John Bridgeman.
By W. Darby.

Lady Charlotte Anne, third daughter of George, second Earl of Bradford ; she died from the effects of being accidentally burnt at Weston Park, 1858. Lady Mary Selina Louisa, the youngest daughter, married, in 1852, the Hon. Robert Clive, M.P., and their son, Robert George, Lord Windsor, succeeded his grandmother, Harriet, Baroness Windsor, in the Barony, 1869. Lord Windsor married, in 1883, Alberta, only daughter of the Right Hon. Sir Augustus Paget, Ambassador at Rome, Vienna, &c., and has issue a son, Other Robert, born 1884, and three other children. The Hon. and Rev. John Robert Orlando, youngest son of George, second Earl of Bradford, is a J.P., Rector of Weston-under-Lizard ; married, in 1862, Marianne Caroline, only child and heiress of the Venerable Archdeacon William Clive, nephew to Robert, the great Lord Clive of Plassey.

498
20in. high × 24in. wide.

Bay Pony belonging to Lucy, Countess of Bradford. *By Smith.*

504
27½in. × 22½

Portrait of a Gentleman. *By Wissing.*

505
43in. × 33½

"*Sine Cerere Baccho friget Venus.*" *After Rubens.*

506
31in. × 43

A Storm at Sea. *By Parcelles.*

508
29½in. × 24½

Colonel Kinnear. *By F. Cotes.*
(Died 1780.) He was Colonel of the 50th Regiment of Foot.

509
In armour.
27in. × 22½

Richard, 2nd Lord Herbert of Cherbury.
(Died 1655.) *By Wissing.*
Son of Edward, first Lord, succeeded in 1648. "Was specially esteemed by King Charles I., for whom he performed many signal services as well with his pen as with his sword." Married Mary, daughter of John, Earl of Bridgewater. His son, Edward, third Lord Herbert, died 1678, without issue, and was succeeded by Henry, fourth Lord Herbert.
(See No. 141.)

510
41in. × 38

St. Catherine disputing with the Doctors.
By Pasqualini.

517
518
519
520
521
522
7½in. × 9¾

Hunting. *By G. Morland.*

523
24in. high x 29in. wide.

A Spaniel.   *By P. Cassteels, 1727.*

531
49in. × 93

Mr. Massey Stanley, with cabriolet and hacks at Hyde Park Corner.   *By Ferneley.*

533
17½in. × 23½

Lord Newport and "Rowton," a favourite hunter, 1862.   *By F. Grant and Ferneley, Senior.*

534
27½in. × 35

Horse and Setters belonging to Orlando, 1st Earl of Bradford, at Stoke Hall, Derbyshire.
By J. Boultbee.

543
29½in. × 24½

Selina, Viscountess Newport, on horseback.
By Sir John Leslie

546
49½in. × 39½

The Master of the Horse's Carriage. Putting=to. 1878.   *By Lutyens.*

548
40in. × 49½

Lady Mabel Bridgeman, on "Claribel."   *By Lutyens.*

553
19½in. × 15½

Viscountess Newport, 1856.   *By F. Grant.*

557
Small Enamel.
6½in. × 5½

S. Rogers, the Poet.

558
6½in. × 5½

W. Wordsworth, the Poet.

585

33½in. high × 51in. wide

A Carp.

Caught in the White Sitch (19lbs. weight) by John Rains, keeper, 1768.

586

Black coat.

21in. diameter.

John George, 2nd Lord Forester.   *By Rothwell.*

(1801—1874.)

Eldest son of the first Lord Forester and Lady Katherine Manners, second daughter of Charles, fourth Duke of Rutland. He married Countess Alexandrina, daughter of Joachim, Count Von Maltzan, of Prussia, and widow of Frederick, third and last Viscount Melbourne.

587

A Gentleman.

588

Small portrait on Panel, labelled "My mother."

Viscountess Torrington.

Lucy Boyle, only daughter of John, fifth Earl of Cork and Orrery. Married George, fourth Viscount Torrington.

589

Small portrait.   Long wig: looking to the left.

A Gentleman.

594

30in. × 46

" Merry Andrew " and " Chillington. "   *By Hopkins.*

595

30in. × 49½

Mares and Foals.   *By W. H. Hopkins, 1889.*

"Duvernay," "White Heather," "Manœuvre," and "Hemlock," with their foals, in the paddock at Weston. "Manœuvre's" foal (by "Wisdom") subsequently named "Sir Hugo," won the Derby in 1892 for the Earl of Bradford.

596

24in. × 29½

" Sir Hugo."   *By W. H. Hopkins, 1892.*

Winner of the Derby, 1892.

597

27½in. × 35½

" Galopin. "   *By Harry Hall, 1875.*

Winner of the Derby, 1875.

599   Shakespeare.

600   A Magdalen.   *By Hayter.*
22in. high × 18in. wide.   Believed to be "Pamela," Lady Campbell, daughter of Lord
Edward Fitzgerald.

601   The Marquis of Granby.   *After Sir J. Reynolds, by H. Hall.*
23in. × 19

602   Landscape, with Cottage.
8in. × 23½

603   " Dangerous."   *By Herring.*
12in. × 16½   Winner of the Derby, 1833.

604   Flowers.

605   Flowers.

607   A Gentleman.
Oval.

608   A Sketch.   *By Rubens.*
21in. × 16¾

609   Orlando George Charles, Earl of Bradford.
23½in. × 17½   In peer's robes.

612   " Mameluke."
27½in. × 35   Winner of the Derby, 1827.

613   Benjamin Disraeli, Earl of Beaconsfield.
13¾in. × 11   *By J. Blake Wirgman, 1877.*
Painted in the Palace of Osborne.

Miniatures.

❦ *Miniatures.* ❧

—:o:—

273   General the Honorable James Ramsay.

By Miss G. E. Moncreiffe.

(1772—1837.)

Third son of the eighth Earl of Dalhousie.

275   Mrs. Henry Tighe.   *By Mrs. Kenyon.*

276   Mary, Queen of Scots.

277   The Honorable Lucy Byng, afterwards Countess
of Bradford.

363   Mary Isabella, Duchess of Rutland.   *By Cosway.*

(1756—1831.)

Daughter of Charles, fourth Duke of Beaufort. Married, in 1775,
Charles, fourth Duke of Rutland, K.G. She was remarkable for her
beauty.

Bio. Cata. p. 239.

402   A Gentleman.

403   A Gentleman.

404   A Lady.

405   A Lady.

58

406   A Lady.

         402—6. These five small miniatures are together in one frame, and were given to the Earl of Bradford by Mr. Shirley, in 1868.

         (The following names are upon paper in the frame :—Mr. Mordaunt, Mr. G. Bridgeman, Louisa Bridgeman.)

407   A Lady with a Harpsichord.

         On a snuff box.

408
Red dress, long wig.   A Gentleman (perhaps Sir O. Bridgeman).

409   Miss Worsley, Heiress of Appuldercombe.

         She was the first wife of the Honorable John Bridgeman Simpson.

412
Reading.   The Hon. Lucy Byng, afterwards Countess of Bradford.

410
White dress, powdered hair.   A young Lady.

411
Powdered hair.   A Lady.

         Miniature, in pearl setting.

413   The Rev. Mr. Chappelow.

414
Lace veil on her head.   Lucy Elizabeth, Countess of Bradford.

415   Josephine, Empress of the French.

416
White dress, with pearl
necklace; in powder.

Elizabeth, Lady Bradford.
On a snuff box.

417
Brown dress; pearls in
her hair.

A Lady.
On a snuff box.

418

The Hon. Elizabeth Bridgeman, afterwards
Mrs. Gunning.
(Died 1810.)
This was left by Sir George Gunning to the Countess of Bradford.

419

A Lady.
On a large ring.

420

A Gentleman.
On a large ring.

421

Mrs. Saltren.

422

The Emperor Alexander II., Czar of Russia.
(1818—1881.)
On the lid of a snuff box. Presented by the Emperor to Orlando,
3rd Earl of Bradford, when Master of the Horse, in May, 1874.

424
With hair slightly
powdered.

Lady John Russell.
Second daughter of Viscount Torrington.

425

Hon. Lucy Byng, Countess of Bradford.

On a brooch which belonged to her sister, Mrs. Seymour, and was given to Lord Bradford by Lady Charles Russell, niece of Mr. Seymour.

426

Hon. Orlando G. C. Bridgeman, 1821.

By Viscountess Newport, after Anthony Stewart.

When two years old. Present Earl of Bradford.

427

A small oval.

Hon. George Byng.

Son of the 4th Viscount Torrington and Lady Lucy Boyle. Died an infant.

428

Yellow Dress.

A Lady.

429

Hon. Orlando and Mrs. Bridgeman, afterwards 1st Earl and Countess of Bradford.

On a snuff box.

430

In blue dress.

A Lady.

Probably Mrs. Bridgeman-Simpson, née Worsley.

431

In brown dress: fur trimming.

A Lady.

432

John Boyle, 5th Earl of Cork and Orrery.

433

On a ring.

Medallion.

434
Trencher cap and college
gown.

Mr. Chappelow, aged 18, afterwards Chaplain to the Earl of Bradford.

435
In white and blue ;
powdered hair.

A Lady, believed to be the Countess of Cork.

436

The German Emperor, William I.

Presented by the Crown Prince and Princess to the third Earl of Bradford when Master of the Horse, March 14th, 1879.

437

A Lady and Cupid.

On enamelled snuff box.

438

The Hon. Orlando Bridgeman, afterwards 1st Earl of Bradford.

439

A Lady, marked as the " Mother of Mary Scott."

Given by Mrs. Scott to the Earl of Bradford in 1844.

440
Black silhouette.

Lady Lucy Bridgeman, daughter of Edmund Boyle, Earl of Cork and Orrery.

441
Black silhouette.

Hon. and Rev. George Bridgeman, son of the 1st Lord Bradford, and husband of the preceding.

442
A circular miniature.

George, 4th Viscount Torrington.

443   **Lady Lucy Whitmore.**

Daughter of Orlando, first Earl of Bradford, by the Hon. Lucy Byng. Married William Wolryche Whitmore, Esq., of Dudmaston, Co. Salop.

444   **General Vandernerck.**

445
&   **The Hon. Mrs. Bridgeman**
446   **and**
        Lady John Russell.

(In one case.)

The Hon. Lucy and the Hon. Georgiana Byng, daughters of Lord Torrington ; the former became afterwards Countess of Bradford, to whom the miniatures were bequeathed by the Duke of Bedford.

447   **Miniature, in a wooden frame.**

448   **The Hon. Isabella Byng, afterwards**
        Marchioness of Bath.

Given to the Countess of Bradford, on her marriage, by the Marquis of Bath.

449   **A Lady with a Lap-dog.**

On the top of an ivory box.

450   **Venus bathing.**

Within the lid of a snuff box, enamelled.

451   **Napoleon Buonaparte.**

(A Medallion.)

452   The Hon. Lucy Byng, afterwards Countess of Bradford.

Small miniature, upon a red snuff box.

454   The Duke of Wellington.

(A Medallion.)

458   Georgina Elizabeth (wife of the 2nd Earl of Bradford), née Moncreiffe.   *After Sir W. Ross.*

466   Georgina Elizabeth, Countess of Bradford.

By W. Ross, 1828.

467   The five eldest children of the 2nd Earl and Countess of Bradford.

By Miss Magdalen Ross, 1828.

468   King George IV.   *By Holmes, after Sir Thomas Lawrence.*

It belonged to the Marquess Conyngham.

469   The Hon. Mrs. Pelham.

(1788—1813.)

Daughter of the Hon. John Bridgeman-Simpson, and heiress of her maternal uncle, Sir Richard Worsley, Bart.   Married the Hon. Charles Pelham, F.R.S., created first Earl of Yarborough.

470   Her Royal Highness the Princess of Wales.

471 Viscount Newport, afterwards 2nd Earl of
Bradford. *By Englehart, 1818.*

472 Georgina Elizabeth, Viscountess Newport, 1819.
By Charlotte Jones.

473 Selina Louisa, Viscountess Newport. *By Thorburn.*

495 The Saviour. *By Georgina, Viscountess Newport.*

497 Sir Orlando Bridgeman, Lord Keeper.
By Miss Caroline Bridgeman-Simpson.
From a picture at Chirk Castle.

499 Lord Clive, 1841.
(A Medallion.)

614 The Hon. O. G. C. Bridgeman, afterwards Earl
of Bradford.
As a child, 1821.

615 The Hon. George Thomas Orlando Bridgeman.
As a child.

616 The Honorable Elizabeth Bridgeman.
As a child. Daughter of George, second Earl of Bradford.

617 Lucy, Countess of Bradford.

618 Lady Mabel S. Bridgeman.

619 Lady Florence K. Bridgeman.

620 The Hon. C. O. Bridgeman, Lieut. in the Navy, 1810.

621 The Hon. G. A. F. H. Bridgeman, Major of the Shropshire Militia, 1810.

622 The Hon. Mrs. Whitmore, 1810.

623 Lord Bradford, as Col. of the Shropshire Militia.

624 Lady Lucy Whitmore.
Black dress.

INDEX.

Subject.	No.	Page.	Painted by
Adoration of the Angels	53	14	
Allegorical	255	45	School of Rubens.
Allegorical (Plenty ?)	167	33	Amiconi.
Allegorical (Peace ?)	169	33	Amiconi.
Allegorical	254	45	School of Rubens.
Angels appearing to the Shepherds... ...	120	23	Giacomo Bassano.
Angel appearing to Joseph, The ...	89	19	G. R. Badaracco.
Annunciation, The	43	12	C. J. Ratti.
Ark, Entering into the	252	45	Ben. Castiglione.
Arundel and Surrey, Earl of	86	19	Sir A. Vandyck.
Bates, The Rev. W., of Willey	278	47	
Battle, A	124	24	Cuyp.
Beaconsfield, Benjamin Disraeli, Earl of ...	613	54	J. Blake Wirgman.
Bedford, Francis Russell, 4th Earl of ...	11	8	Remé.
Bedford, William Russell, 5th Earl, 1st Duke of ...	16	8	Sir G. Kneller.
Birds	94	20	Van Kessel or " Boon."
Bradford, The Countess of	156	31	Clifford.
Bradford, Lady Diana Russell, 1st Countess of ...	51	13	
Bradford, The Earl of (Leicestershire scene) ..	313	47	Ferneley.
Bradford, The Earl of, F. Gillard, and Hounds	316	48	F. Grant.
Bradford, Elizabeth. Lady	162	32	Pine.
Bradford, Elizabeth, Lady	262	46	Sir Wm. Ross.
Bradford, Elizabeth, Lady	214	40	
Bradford, Elizabeth, Lady	416	59	
Bradford, Five Children of 2nd Earl and Countess of ...	467	63	Miss Magdalen Ross.
Bradford, Francis, Earl of	148	28	M. Dahl.
Bradford, George A. F. H., 2nd Earl of ...	66	16	Sir George Hayter.
Bradford, George A. F. H., 2nd Earl of ...	199	38	Sir George Hayter, R.A.
Bradford, Georgina Elizabeth, Countess of ...	458	63	After Sir W. Ross.
Bradford, Georgina, Countess of	466	63	W. Ross, 1828.
Bradford, Henry, 1st Lord	80	18	Romney.
Bradford, Henry, Viscount Newport, Earl of...	139	26	M. Dahl.
Bradford, Henry, Lord	215	40	
Bradford, Lord, as Colonel of the Shropshire Militia ...	628	65	
Bradford, Lucy E., Dowager Countess of ..	229	42	Sir Wm. Ross.
Bradford, Lucy Elizabeth, Countess of ...	414	58	
Bradford, Lucy, Countess of	617	64	
Bradford, Mary, Countess of	134	25	J. M. Wright.
Bradford, Orlando, 1st Earl of	68	16	Sir George Hayter.
Bradford, Orlando Bridgeman, 1st Earl of ...	173	34	Pine.
Bradford, Orlando G. C., 3rd Earl of ...	201	39	Sir Francis Grant.
Bradford, Orlando G. C., Earl of	609	54	
Bradford, Richard Newport, 2nd Earl of	185	26	Sir Peter Lely.
Bradford, Hon. Selina Forester, afterwards Countess of	62	15	Sir Francis Grant.
Bradford, Hon. Selina Forester, afterwards Countess of	210	40	Sir F. Grant, P.R.A.

Subject.	No.	Page.	Painted by
Bridgeman, Bishop, Scene from Life of	393	50	*Cattermole.*
Bridgeman, Ladies C. and M., and Hon. John ...	496	50	*W. Darby.*
Bridgeman, Hon. C. O., Lieutenant, R.N.	620	65	
Bridgeman, Captain the Hon. Charles, R.N.	61	15	*Sir George Hayter.*
Bridgeman, Miss Diana	158	31	*F. Cotes.*
Bridgeman, Doctor John, Bishop of Chester	187	26	*C. Jansen.*
Bridgeman, Hon. Elizabeth, afterwards Mrs. Gunning	418	59	
Bridgeman, Hon. Elizabeth	616	64	
Bridgeman, Lady Florence K.	619	65	
Bridgeman, The Hon. and Rev. George	75	17	*Constable.*
Bridgeman, Mr. George	81	18	*Sir Joshua Reynolds.*
Bridgeman, Mr. George, afterwards 2nd Earl of Bradford	270	46	
Bridgeman, The Hon. G. T. O.	615	64	
Bridgeman, Hon. and Rev. George	441	61	
Bridgeman, Hon. George C. O.	330	47	
Bridgeman, Hon. Gerald O. M.	390	59	*Lundgren.*
Bridgeman, Hon. G. A. F. H., Major	621	65	
Bridgeman, Hon. Mrs., and Lady John Russell ⎱⎰	445 & 446	62	
Bridgeman, Sir Henry, and Family	147	29	*Pine.*
Bridgeman, Hon. Henry Edmund	231	42	*Sharples.*
Bridgeman, Sir John, 3rd Baronet	142	28	*Closterman.*
Bridgeman, John, Bishop of Chester	190	36	*Van Somers.*
Bridgeman, Sir John, 2nd Baronet	146	29	*J. Vitors.*
Bridgeman, Lord-Keeper	136	26	*Sir Peter Lely.*
Bridgeman, Lady Lucy	440	61	
Bridgeman, Mrs.	149	30	*C. Jansen.*
Bridgeman, Mr., of Devonshire	157	31	
Bridgeman, Mrs., of Devonshire ... ··· ...	160	32	
Bridgeman, Miss, afterwards Hon. Mrs. Lewis ...	152	30	
Bridgeman, Lady Mabel, on " Claribel "	548	52	*Lutyens.*
Bridgeman, Lady Mabel	329	47	*E. Clifford.*
Bridgeman, Hon. M. and F.	387	49	*A. Blackley.*
Bridgeman, Lady Mabel	618	65	
Bridgeman, Sir Orlando	3	5	*Riley.*
Bridgeman, Hon. Orlando	60	15	*Sir George Hayter.*
Bridgeman, Hon. O. G. C.	88	18	*Sir George Hayter.*
Bridgeman, Orlando, Esq.	151	30	*M. Dahl.*
Bridgeman, Sir O., 4th Baronet	138	26	*Vanderbank.*
Bridgeman, Sir O., 4th Baronet	175	34	*F. Cotes.*
Bridgeman, Orlando, Esq., afterwards 1st Earl of Bradford	235	43	
Bridgeman, Orlando, Esq., afterwards 1st Earl of Bradford	236	43	
Bridgeman, Hon. O. and H., as Cherubs	493	50	
Bridgeman, Hon. O. G. C., afterwards Earl of Bradford	614	64	
Bridgeman, Hon. O., afterwards 1st Earl of Bradford ...	438	61	
Bridgeman, Hon. O. and Mrs., afterwards 1st Earl and Countess of Bradford	429	60	
Bridgeman, Hon. Orlando G. C., 1821	426	60	*Viscountess Newport, after Anthony Stewart.*

Subject.	No.	Page.	Painted by
Bridgeman, Sir O., Lord-Keeper	497	64	*Miss C. Bridgeman-Simpson.*
Bridgeman-Simpson, Hon. John	76	17	*After Hoppner.*
Bridgeman-Simpson, Hon. Mrs.	232	42	
Bridgeman, Ursula, Lady...	183	35	
Butler, Author of " Hudibras "	267	46	
Byng, Hon. George	427	60	
Byng, Hon. Isabella, afterwards Marchioness of Bath ...	448	62	
Byng, Hon. Lucy, afterwards Countess of Bradford ...	271	46	
Byng, Hon. Lucy, afterwards Countess of Bradford ...	277	57	
Byng, Hon. Lucy, afterwards Countess of Bradford ...	412	58	
Byng, Hon. Lucy, afterwards Countess of Bradford ...	425	60	
Byng, Hon. Lucy, afterwards Countess of Bradford ...	452	63	
Cabaret, Inside of a	32	11	*Brower.*
Cadmus and the Dragon	30	11	*Paul Brill.*
Calm, A	118	23	*J. Vernet.*
Carew, Sir Nicholas	109	22	*Holbein.*
Carlisle, Margaret Howard, Countess of, and her Niece	84	19	*Stone, after Vandyck.*
Carp, A, 1768	585	53	
Castle Bromwich Hall	343	48	*Everitt.*
Chappelow, Rev. Leonard...	234	43	*Sharples.*
Chappelow, Mr.	434	61	
Chappelow, Rev. L.	413	58	
Charles I., King of England	90	20	*Carlo Maratti, after Vandyck.*
Cherub, A	91	20	*Paul Veronese.*
Cherub, A	93	20	*Paul Veronese.*
Chesterfield, Anne E., Countess of	391	50	*Miss Cruickshank, after Sir E. Landseer.*
China	216	40	*Roestraeten.*
Clive, Lord, 1841	499		
Continence of Scipio	170	33	*Simon de Vos.*
Conyngham, Lady Albert...	354	48	*F. Grant.*
Cork and Orrery, John Boyle, 5th Earl of	432	60	
Council of War, A	177	35	*Leandro Bassano.*
Creation, The	212	40	*Hondt.*
Cromwell, Lord	127	24	*Holbein.*
Cross, Taking down from the	71	16	*Palma Vecchio.*
Crown of Thorns, The	242	44	
Crucifixion, The...	44	12	*Bernardo Strozzi, called " Il Capucino."*
Cupid reclining	132	25	*Guido Reni.*
Cupid shaving his Bow	92	20	*After Correggio.*
Dædalus and Icarus	125	24	*Paul Brill.*
Dalhousie, The Marquess of	200	39	*G. F. Clarke, after Sir J. Watson Gordon.*
Danaë and the Golden Shower	38	12	*J. Rothenhamer.*
" Dangerous," winner of the Derby, 1833	603	54	*Herring.*
Davis, Mrs.	166	33	*Sir Peter Lely.*
Derby, Edward Stanley, 14th Earl of	72	16	*Sir Francis Grant, P.R.A.*

SUBJECT.	No.	PAGE.	PAINTED BY
Diana and her Nymphs	258	45	*School of Rubens.*
Digby, Sir Kenelm	119	23	*Vandyck.*
Dog, A large, with Jacobe	185	35	*Weaver.*
Dogs and Game	128	25	*David de Koninck.*
Dogs, Three	197	38	*G. W. Horlor.*
Dormer, Lady Elizabeth, afterwards Countess of Mountrath	55	14	*Sir Peter Lely.*
Dysart, Grace, Countess of	133	25	*Sir G. Kneller.*
Dysart, Lionel T., 2nd Earl of	154	31	
Emperor Alexander II., Czar of Russia	422	59	
Empress of the French, Josephine ...	415	58	
Emperor, William I., The German ...	436	61	
Esther and Ahasuerus	98	21	*Ehrenberg.*
Female Figures, Skull, and Cupid ...	217	40	*After Domenichino.*
Fielding, Lady Diana	56	14	*Sir Peter Lely.*
Flight into Egypt, The	21	9	*Castiglione.*
Flight into Egypt, The	49	13	*Filippo Lauri.*
Flight into Egypt, The	85	19	*G. Raf. Badaracco.*
Flowers	604	54	
Flowers	605	54	
Forester, George, Esq.	188	36	
Forester, John George, 2nd Lord ...	586	53	*Rothwell.*
Fruit	211	40	*De Heem.*
Fruit	224	41	*De Heem.*
Fruit and Flowers	253	45	*Campidoglio.*
Flowers and Fruit	257	45	*Campidoglio.*
" Galopin " winner of the Derby, 1875	597	53	*Harry Hall.*
Game of Rouge et Noir, A ...	31	11	*Molenaer.*
Gentleman, A	402	57	
Gentleman, A	403	57	
Gentleman, A	408	58	
Gentleman, A	420	59	
Gentleman, A	587	53	
Gentleman, A	589	53	
Gentleman, A	607	54	
Gentleman, A	116	23	*Titian.*
Gentleman, A	171	34	*Philip de Koning*
Glaucus and Scylla	249	45	*Filippo Lauri.*
Goring, Colonel, afterwards Lord ...	46	13	*After Vandyck.*
Granby, The Marquis of	601	54	*After Sir J. Reynolds, by H. Hall.*
Grotius, Hugo	5	7	*Mirevelt.*
Gunning, Sir George, Baronet	77	17	*J. Jackson.*
Gunning, The Hon. Mrs. ...	148	29	*Hoppner.*
Hamet Ben Hamet	218	41	*Sir G. Kneller.*
Harvey, William, M.D.	14	8	
Head of John the Baptist, The ...	104	21	
Head, A Man's	111	22	*Tintoretto.*

SUBJECT.					No.	PAGE.	PAINTED BY
Herbert of Cherbury, Henry, 4th Lord	...		...	...	141	27	*Wissing.*
Herbert, Mistress	...	...	...	...	126	24	*Zucchero.*
Herbert of Cherbury, Richard, 2nd Lord	...		...	...	509	51	*Wissing.*
Hippomenes and Atalanta	...		...	...	87	19	*F. Albano.*
Holland, Henry Rich, Earl of	...		...	...	191	37	*Henry Stone.*
Holy Scripture, Six Subjects from	...		...	...	259	46	*Pietro Perugino.*
Horses, Two	...	...	...	...	...	8	7	*Stubbs.*
Horse, A Lean White	...	...	...	...	213	40	*Peter de Laer.*
Horse and Setters of Orlando, 1st Earl of Bradford, at							
Stoke Hall	...	...	...	...	...	534	52	*J. Boultbee.*
Hunting	...	...	...	...	...	517	51	*G. Morland.*
Hunting	...	...	...	...	...	518	51	*G. Morland.*
Hunting	...	...		...	...	519	51	*G. Morland.*
Hunting	...	...		...	...	520	51	*G. Morland.*
Hunting	...	...		...	...	521	51	*G. Morland.*
Hunting	...	...		...	...	522	51	*G. Morland.*
Interior, with Figures				...	272	46	
Italian Children				...	358	49	*G. Fortunati.*
Jacob at the Well	...	...		...	172	34	*Francesco Bassano.*
Jesus calling St. Peter out of the Boat				...	121	24	*Breughel.*
Jesus casting out Devils	...	...		...	245	44	*Paul Brill.*
Judgment of Paris, The	...			...	96	20	*Poëlemburg.*
Jupiter and Io	...	...		...	50	13	*Filippo Lauri.*
Killigrew, Lady	...	...		...	129	25	*Vandyck.*
Killigrew, Sir Thomas	...		...		...	123	24	*Vandyck.*
Kinnear, Colonel	...		...		...	508	51	*F. Cotes.*
Kingston, The Countess of			...		...	226	41	*Mrs. Beale.*
King George II	...		...		...	70	16	*Pine.*
King George IV	...		...		...	468	63	*Holmes, after Sir Thomas Lawrence.*
Lady, A	...	...	...	...	...	58	14	*Sir Peter Lely.*
Lady, A	...	...	...	...	...	59	14	*Sir Peter Lely.*
Lady, A	...	...	...	...	...	99	21	*Lucas Cranach.*
Lady with a Monkey and Flower Pot, A		...		...	101	21	*Paris Bordone.*
Lady, A	...	...	...	...	...	168	33	*Sir Antonio More.*
Lady, A	...	...	...	...	...	178	35	*G. Murphy.*
Lady, Portrait of a Young		...		...	155	31	*Mrs. Beale.*
Lady, A	...	...	...	...	...	404	57	
Lady, A	...	...	...	...	...	405	57	
Lady, A	...	...	...	...	...	406	58	
Lady, A, with a Harpsichord		...		...	407	58	
Lady, A young	...	...	...	...	...	410	58	
Lady, A	..	...	...	...	...	411	58	
Lady, A	..	...	...	...	...	417	58	
Lady, A	...	...	...	...	...	419	59	
Lady, A	...	...	...	...	...	428	60	
Lady, A	...	...	...	...	...	430	60	
Lady, A	...	...	...	...	...	431	60	
Lady, A, believed to be the Countess of Cork				...	435	61	

Subject.	No.	Page.	Painted by
Lady and Cupid, A	437	61	
Lady, A, " Mother of Mary Scott "...	489	61	
Lady, A, with a Lap-dog	449	62	
Landscape	23	10	*Berghem.*
Landscape	25	10	*Bout and Bodewyns.*
Landscape, with a Philosopher studying	27	10	*Joachim Patenier.*
Landscape	29	10	*Berghem.*
Landscape, with Figures	42	12	*Salvator Rosa.*
Landscape, A	47	13	*Claude Lorraine.*
Landscape, A	240	43	*Old Breughel.*
Landscape and Figures	241	44	*Peter Breydel.*
Landscape, A	243	44	*Peter de Laer.*
Landscape, A	256	45	*School of Rembrandt.*
Landscape, A	290	47	*Charles. 6th Duke of Rutland.*
Landscape and Figures, A ...	239	43	*Peter Breydel.*
Landscape, with Cottage	602	54	
Landscape, " Honister Crag " ...	186	35	
Landscape, " Langdale " ...	184	35	
Landscape, with a Pack-Horse ...	163	32	*Rosa da Tivoli.*
Landscape, with a Shower of Rain ...	164	32	*Lankrink.*
Landscape, with Cattle and Sheep ...	344	48	*Cooper.*
Landscape	382	49	*Claude Lorraine.*
Larder Scene, with Dogs	107	22	*Snyders.*
Lewis, H. Greswold, Esq. ...	74	17	*Constable.*
Lichfield Cathedral	347	48	*Fernyhough.*
Liverpool, Robert Jenkinson, 2nd Earl of	64	15	*Sir George Hayter.*
Londesborough, Lord and Lady	293 294	47	*F. Grant.*
Lowther, Sir William, Baronet ...	78	17	*Sir Joshua Reynolds.*
Madonna with Sleeping Child	20	9	*Gio André de Ferrari.*
Madonna	24	10	*Sasso Ferrato.*
Madonna, A	297	43	*Venetian School.*
Magdalen, A	600	54	*Hayter.*
" Mameluke," winner of the Derby, 1827 ...	612	54	
Maria Christina, Archduchess of Austria ...	244	44	
Mares and Foals, 1889	595	53	*W. H. Hopkins.*
Mary, Queen of Scots	165	33	
Mary, Queen of Scots	276	57	
Master of the Horse's Carriage, 1878 ...	546	52	*Lutyens.*
Medallion	433	60	
" Merry Andrew " and " Chillington " ...	594	53	*Hopkins.*
Miniature, in wooden frame	447	62	
Moonlight Scene, A	100	21	*Vanderneer.*
Moncreiffe, Sir Thomas, and his sister Helen ..	233	43	*Sir Wm. Ross.*
Moncreiffe, Sir David, Baronet	269	46	
Music Lesson, A	35	11	*W. Mieris.*
Myddleton, Sir Thomas	17	9	*Russell.*
Myddleton, Lady	198	38	

Subject.	No.	Page.	Painted by
Napoleon Buonaparte, 1st Emperor of France ...	65	15	*David.*
Napoleon Buonaparte	451	62	
Nell Gwynne	176	34	*Mrs. Beale.*
Newport, Viscountess, 1856	553	52	*F. Grant.*
Newport, Selina, Viscountess, on horseback ...	543	52	*Sir John Leslie.*
Newport, Diana, Viscountess, afterwards Countess of Bradford	57	14	*Verelst.*
Newport, Selina Louisa, Viscountess ...	248	44	*James Swinton.*
Newport, Orlando G. C., Viscount	247	44	*James Swinton.*
Newport, The Hon. Colonel Andrew ...	6	7	*Sir Godfrey Kneller.*
Newport, Lady Anne	140	27	*Vanderbank.*
Newport, Lady Mary	161	32	*Mrs. Beale.*
Newport, Francis, 2nd Baron	187	36	*Sir Godfrey Kneller.*
Newport, Francis, 1st Earl of Bradford ...	192	37	*After Dahl.*
Newport, Viscount, 1840	494	50	
Newport, Lord, and "Rowton," 1862 ...	533	52	*F. Grant & Ferneley, Sen.*
Newport, Viscount, afterwards 2nd Earl of Bradford ...	471	64	*Englehart.*
Newport, Georgina Elizabeth, Viscountess ...	472	64	*Charlotte Jones.*
Newport, Selina L., Viscountess ...	473	64	*Thorburn.*
Noah entering the Ark	208	39	*Hondt.*
" *Noli Me tangere* "	52	13	*Carlo Maratti.*
Nymph and Satyr, A	102	21	*Poëlemburg.*
Offer rejected, An	39	12	*W. Mieris.*
Old Woman with an Hour Glass, An ...	37	11	*Gerard Dow.*
Old Man's Head, An	110	22	*Vandyck.*
Oxford, Beatrix, Countess of ...	113	22	*Vandyck.*
Parrot and Flowers	221	41	*Verelst.*
Payne, Admiral	82	18	*Hoppner.*
Pelham, Hon. Mrs.	469	63	
Piper, A	117	23	*Piazetti, after Giorgione.*
Pony, Bay, belonging to Lucy, Countess of Bradford ...	498	51	*Smith.*
Porter, Lady	196	38	*Hale.*
Portrait	68	15	
Portrait of a Child	105	21	*Paul Veronese.*
Portrait of a Child	108	22	*Paul Veronese.*
Portrait of a Gentleman	116	23	*Titian.*
Portrait of a Lady	168	33	*Sir Antonio More.*
Portrait of a Gentleman	171	34	*Philip de Koning.*
Portrait of a Lady	178	35	*G. Murphy.*
Portrait of a Gentleman	182	35	
Portrait of a Gentleman	189	36	
Portrait of a Gentleman	504	51	*Wissing.*
Princess of Wales, H.R.H.	470	63	
Prince Maurice, as Cupid	19	9	*Honthorst.*
Prince Rupert, as Mars	48	13	*Honthorst.*
Queen Anne Boleyn (A Sketch)	67	16	*Holbein.*
Queen Victoria, Her Majesty	69	16	*Thomas.*
Queen Victoria, Her Majesty	220	41	*J. Blake Wirgman.*
Queen Victoria, Her Majesty	251	45	*Clarke, after Winterhalter*

SUBJECT.	No.	PAGE.	PAINTED BY
Queen Victoria, Her Majesty	355	48	*G. Thomas.*
Queen, The, at Prince of Wales' Marriage, 1863 ...	378	49	*Thomas.*
Ramsay, General the Hon. James	273	57	*Miss G. E. Moncreiffe.*
Rembrandt	265	46	
Rhine, View on the	131	25	*Herman Sachtleven.*
Rogers, S., the Poet	557	52	
Rubens	266	16	
Russell, Rachel, Lady	1	5	
Russell, Hon. Edward	15	8	*Remé.*
Russell, Lady Robert	2	5	*Sir G. Kneller.*
Russell, Lord Robert	4	7	*Sir G. Kneller.*
Russell, Hon. Francis	18	9	*Remé.*
Russell, Colonel the Hon. John	10	7	*Sir G. Kneller.*
Russell, Lord John	230	42	*Sir G. Hayter.*
Russell, William, Lord	13	8	*Russell.*
Russell, Lady John	424	59	
Russell, Lady John	446	62	
Russell, Lady Diana, 1st Countess of Bradford ...	51	13	
Rutland, Mary Isabella, Duchess of ...	363	57	*Cosway.*
St. Catherine disputing with the Doctors ...	510	51	*Pasqualini.*
St. Catherine	41	12	*E. Sirani.*
St. Peter, St. James, and St. John...	7	7	*Caravaggio.*
St. Peter walking on the Sea ...	115	23	*J. Breughet.*
St. Sebastian, The Martyrdom of ...	209	39	*Jacques Callot.*
St. Catherine, Virgin and Martyr ...	246	44	*After Domenichino.*
St. Lawrence, Martyrdom of ...	274	46	
Saltren, Mrs.	421	59	
Saviour, The	495	64	*Georgina, Viscountess Newport.*
Saviour, Our, and St. John ...	22	9	*Peter van Lindt.*
Saviour, The, bearing the Cross ...	122	24	*Paul Veronese.*
Saviour, The, betrayed by Judas ...	238	43	*Guercino.*
Sea piece, A	33	11	*Abraham Stork.*
Sea piece, with Ships sailing, A ...	130	25	*Vandervelde.*
Sea Sketch	357	48	*Copley Fielding.*
Seneca instructing Nero	12	8	*Spanish School.*
Seymour, Lord Hugh, Vice-Admiral ...	79	18	*Hoppner.*
Shakespeare	599	54	
"Sir Hugo," winner of the Derby, 1892 ...	596	53	*W. H. Hopkins.*
"Sine Cerere Baccho friget Venus" ...	505	51	*After Rubens.*
Sketch, A	608	54	*Rubens.*
Sleeping Venus	179	35	*After Titian.*
Somerset, Sir Edward Seymour, Duke of ...	97	20	*Holbein.*
Southampton, Thomas Wriothesley, Earl of ...	84	11	*Sir Peter Lely.*
Spaniel, A	523	52	*P. Casteels.*
Spoils of War	180	35	
Strafford, Thomas Wentworth, Earl of, and his Secretary	9	7	*After Vandyck.*
Storm, A	112	22	*Joseph Vernet.*
Storm at Sea	506	51	*Parcelles.*
Stanley, Mr. Massey, with cabriolet and hacks ...	581	52	*Ferneley.*

Subject.		No.	Page.	Painted by
Subjects, Eight, from the History of Our Saviour	...	45	12	*Flavio Minaresi.*
Sunderland, Dorothy, Countess of	...	88	19	*Vandyck.*
Supper, A	...	250	45	*Cornelius de Waal.*
Swiss brandishing his Sword, A	...	28	10	*Bol.*
Sybil, A	...	40	12	*Schidone.*
Tighe, Mrs. Henry	...	275	57	*Mrs. Kenyon.*
Topers	...	36	11	*Teniers.*
Torrington, George, 4th Viscount	...	442	61	
Torrington, George Byng, 4th Viscount ...	...	174	34	*Ramsay.*
Torrington, 4th Viscount...	...	268	46	*A. D. Hamilton.*
Torrington, Lucy, Viscountess	...	153	30	*Gainsborough.*
Torrington, Viscountess	...	588	58	
Turenne, Marshal	...	198	37	
Two Boys playing	...	181	35	*Vandyck.*
Vandernerck, General	...	444	62	
Vandyck, as Paris	...	106	22	*After Vandyck.*
Venetian Courtesan, A	...	95	20	*Paul Veronese.*
Venus bathing	...	450	62	
Venus and Cupid	...	54	14	*Filippo Lauri.*
Venus giving Arms to Æneas	...	103	21	*Venetian School.*
Villiers, Ladies S. and C....	...	322	47	*Chalon.*
Virgin and Child	...	388	49	*Italian.*
Virgin and Child	...	219	41	*School of Correggio.*
Virgin and Child, with St. John	...	73	16	*Sotto Cleve.*
Warwick, Charlotte, Countess of ...	...	159	32	*Sir Godfrey Kneller.*
Wellington, The Duke of	...	206	39	*Hayter and Wm. Proctor.*
Wellington, The Duke of	...	223	41	*Sir George Hayter.*
Wellington, The Duke of	...	454	63	
West, Colonel	...	26	10	*Walker.*
Whitmore, Hon. Mrs., 1810 ...	...	622	65	
Whitmore, Lady Lucy	...	443	62	
Whitmore, Lady Lucy	...	624	65	
Wilbraham, Lady	...	144	28	*Sir P. Lely*
Wilbraham, Sir Thomas	...	145	29	*Verelst.*
Windermere, Head of	...	356	48	*Glover.*
Winter Scene, A	...	114	23	*Francesco Bassano.*
Woman bathing, A	...	150	30	*Simon Voët.*
Wordsworth, W., the Poet ...	...	558	52	
Worsley, Miss, Heiress of Appuldercombe	...	409	58	
Yates, Mary ...	...	225	41	*Colombo.*

www.ingramcontent.com/pod-product-compliance
Lightning Source LLC
Chambersburg PA
CBHW021526270326
41930CB00008B/1119